DOUGHNUT
COOKBOOK FOR BEGINNERS

100+ Easy and Delicious Doughnut Recipes Ready for Your
Oven and Doughnut Maker to Match Every Craving.

No Fryer Required!

MARA BAKER

TABLE OF CONTENTS

INTRODUCTION

Doughnuts are ruling the hearts since the 1800s. Have you ever wondered how these sweet and fluffy rings came into existence? Well, it all started when a 16-year-old Hanson Gregory showed disliking towards the greasiness and raw center of regular doughnuts.

Therefore, to make the doughnuts match his taste buds, he pocked a hole into the dough. That's how the doughnuts, the world is crazy about were created. Additionally, the issue of the dough being oily and uncooked center was resolved.

Thanks to Hanson, we can enjoy the delicious and perfectly gooey doughnuts today. Doughnuts are a kind of fried dough served as a dessert food. They are the talk of the town in numerous countries and are cooked in different faces.

You can find them as a homemade sweet snack complementing your evening tea or coffee to occasional treats on birthdays and parties. Doughnuts have kids as their big investors as they are colorful, delicious, and look highly appealing when decorated.

Where there is a worldwide fan following of the tempting and scrumptious doughnuts, we have done you good. You must want to learn how these small chunks of goodness are made.

Nothing feels better than a batch of fresh doughnuts made from scratch in your kitchen. How calming will it be that the cool breeze is blowing from your kitchen window and your doughnuts are ready to be baked? Warm and soft.

Therefore, we've come up with this efficient cooking guide for you. It has a plethora of doughnut recipes, compiled with different ideas and disparate parts of the world. In short, we have gathered a huge variety under one book. It's a one-stop solution for you.

No need to worry about the toppings and add-ons, we have got you covered. These wonderful recipes will help you create delicious doughnuts, doughnut holes, fritters, crullers, and more. Without any further ado, we have compiled a few tips that you may need to learn before getting to work.

Hastes makes waste. Therefore, be patient. The yeast can take time to rise depending on the temperature. Never heat yeast.

Less flour makes tender and soft doughnuts. More flour creates a caky texture (which is also excellent). You'll know that the dough is ready if an indention remains after poking your dough with a finger.

Dust the flour over your doughnut cutter before use, it prevents sticking. Also, steel doughnut cutters offer an even size cut each time. 3"-4" lengths. You can also improvise with a biscuit cutter.

Canola oil is an excellent choice for frying, but peanut oil has a higher smoking point and is also the right choice. Otherwise, for fantastic taste, go with Crisco or solid shortening, if the recipe allows. Aim for a minimum of 1-2" oil depth for frying.

High sides are best for doughnut making. Deep fryers, Dutch ovens, and stockpots work well. Keep the kiddies out of the kitchen for safety.

375°F is the typical temperature for the oil. You can check using a thermometer or a day-old cube of bread. If the bread becomes brown within 60 seconds, you can be assured the oil is ready.

Slide doughnuts gently into oil to prevent splatter. Dropping doughnut batter into hot fat eliminates the need to roll and cut, but be sure to do so carefully and close to the oil. Avoid falling from high, and take care not to burn yourself (or others).

Fry only as many doughnuts at one time as can float quickly in oil or shortening. Overcrowding will not produce good results.

When turning or lifting doughnuts, take extra care not to pierce them. This will allow additional oil to seep in and ruin your finished treat.

For draining excess oil or glazing, cover a large portion of a countertop with wax paper or paper towels and top with a wire cooling rack.

Keep all these tried and tested tricks in your heart and rock the doughnut's cooking game. Let it be cooking or baking the doughnuts, it has become easy with our cookbook. What are you waiting for? Scroll down.

CHAPTER 1: CHOCOLATE BAKED DOUGHNUT RECIPES

1. MOM'S MAGICAL ALMOND DONUTS WITH CHOCOLATE GLAZE

Preparation Time: 5 minutes
Cooking Time: 17 minutes
Servings: 8

Ingredients:

- 1/3 cup powdered Stevia
- ¼ cup butter
- 1/3 cup cocoa powder
- A pinch of sea salt
- ¾ cup packed wheat flour
- ½ tsp apple cider vinegar
- ¼ tsp baking soda
- Ingredients for making chocolate glaze:
- 2 tbsp butter
- 1 oz unsweetened chocolate
- 3 tbsp powdered Stevia

Directions:

1. Keep the oven ready by preheating at 350 degrees and grease the donut pan with cooking spray.
2. Blend the butter with Stevia over low heat and then add the other donut making a smooth batter.
3. Pour the batter into a donut pan and bake them for 15 minutes.
4. Make the chocolate glaze by melting the chocolate in a double boiler and then add the other ingredients, making sure that the sweetener dissolves completely.
5. Spread the coating over the donuts and let them set properly before serving.

Nutritional Information:

Protein: 3.2g; Fat: 6.9g; Carbohydrate: 2.1g

2. PROTEIN BOMB CHOCOLATE DONUTS

Preparation Time: 3 minutes
Cooking Time: 12 minutes
Servings: 12

Ingredients:

- ¾ cup whole grain flour
- 1 tsp baking powder
- ¾ cup wheat flour
- ¼ cup egg whites
- 1 tbsp canola oil
- ½ tsp cinnamon
- ½ tsp baking soda
- 3 tbsp stevia
- ½ cup cocoa powder
- 3 tbsp cocoa powder
- 1/3 cup water

Ingredients for making top coating:

- ½ tsp vanilla extract
- ¼ cup chocolate (semi-sweet)
- 2 tsp coconut milk (unsweetened)

Directions:

1. Keep the oven ready by preheating it at 325 degrees.
2. Put the wheat flour, cocoa powder, whole grain flour, baking soda, baking powder, cinnamon, cocoa powder, and stevia in a bowl and blend thoroughly. Now add the wet ingredients one by one.
3. A hand blender can be used to make the batter smooth. Pour the batter into the donut pan and bake them for 8 minutes.
4. Make the top coating by melting the chocolate chips in a microwave oven and blend in the other ingredients. Spread the top layer over the donuts and let them stand for some time to set the coating.

Nutritional Information:

Protein: 7.5g; Fat: 5.4g; Carbohydrate: 9.1g

3. CHOCO-CHOCO ICY DONUTS

Preparation Time: 5 minutes
Cooking Time: 25 minutes
Servings: 8

Ingredients:

- ¼ cup shredded coconut
- ½ cup coconut flour
- ¼ tsp salt
- ¼ tsp baking soda
- 1 tbsp vanilla extract
- ½ cup of coconut oil
- ¼ unsweetened almond milk
- Six eggs
- ¼ cup Stevia
- ¼ tsp stevia extract powder

Ingredients for making icing:

- ½ tsp vanilla extract
- ¼ cup butter
- ¼ tsp stevia extract powder
- ¼ cup unsweetened almond milk
- 6 tbsp cocoa powder
- ¼ cup powdered Stevia

Directions:

1. Mix the dry and wet ingredients separately and then blend them to make the donut batter.
2. Pour the batter into a greased donut pan and bake them for 20 minutes at 350 degrees.
3. To make the icing, mix all the ingredients thoroughly to make a smooth paste and spread it over the donuts.
4. Let them stand for some time so that the icing can set.

Nutritional Information:

Protein: 2g; Fat: 11g; Carbohydrate: 6g

4. CHOCOLATE MAGIC DONUTS WITH PEANUT BUTTER AND SALTED CARAMEL

Preparation Time: 3 minutes
Cooking Time: 15 minutes
Servings: 5

Ingredients for making chocolate donuts:

- 3 tbsp cocoa powder
- 2 tbsp butter
- 1 tsp vanilla extract
- ½ tsp instant coffee granules
- ¼ tsp cream of tartar
- ¼ tsp cornstarch
- 2 tbsp coconut flour
- ¼ tsp baking soda
- One egg
- ¼ cup granulated Stevia
- 2 tbsp water
- ¼ tsp liquid stevia

Ingredients for making peanut butter frosting:

- 2 tbsp Stevia
- 1 tbsp butter
- 2 tbsp creamy peanut butter
- Ingredients for salted caramel drizzle:
- 1 tbsp Stevia
- 1 tsp maple syrup
- 2 tbsp salted butter

Directions:

1. Put the Stevia, butter, coffee, and cocoa in a saucepan and stir them continuously on medium heat, making sure that the Stevia dissolves completely.
2. Remove the pan from heat and then add the vanilla extract, water, and stevia. Allow a bit of cooling and then mix the egg, followed by combining cream of tartar, coconut flour, cornstarch, and baking soda. Make the batter smooth.
3. Pour the batter into a greased donut pan and bake at 375 degrees for 9 minutes.
4. Place them on the cooling rack for some time.
5. To make the peanut butter frosting, all the ingredients are to be blended in a pan over medium heat and then pour the mixture into a cream pipe.
6. Now make the salted caramel by mixing the ingredients over medium heat and transfer the mixture into another piping bag.
7. Coat the top of the donut with peanut frosting and then with the salted caramel. Let the coatings set for a few minutes and then serve.

Nutritional Information:

Protein: 3.6g; Fat: 13.3g; Carbohydrate: 2.6g

5. SEATTLE CHOCOLATE DONUTS (VEGAN)

Preparation Time: 1 hour
Cooking Time: 1 hour 30 minutes
Servings: 30

Ingredients:

- 1 1/2 C. granulated beet sugar
- 1 egg
- 4 tbsp non-hydrogenated vegan margarine
- 4 oz. unsweetened baking chocolate
- 1 1/2 tsp pure vanilla extract
- 1 C. soy milk, mixed with 1 tsp white vinegar
- 3 1/2 C. unbleached flour
- 3 tsp baking powder
- 1 tsp baking soda
- 1/2 tsp salt

Directions:

1. In a bowl, add the sugar and the egg replacer and beat until creamy.
2. In a pan, add the chocolate and margarine over low heat and cook until melted completely, stirring continuously.
3. Remove from the heat and keep aside to cool.
4. Add the chocolate mixture into the sugar mixture and beat until well combined.

5. In another bowl, add the vinegar, soy milk, and vanilla and mix well.
6. Add the vinegar mixture into the chocolate mixture and mix well.
7. In a third bowl, add the flour, baking soda, baking powder, and salt and mix well.
8. Add the flour mixture into the chocolate mixture and mix until a dough forms.
9. Refrigerate for about 30 minutes.
10. Place the dough onto a floured surface and roll into 1/2-inch thickness.
11. With a doughnut cutter, cut the doughnuts.
12. Keep aside for about 10 minutes.
13. In a deep skillet, add the oil and cook until heated through.
14. Add the doughnuts in batches and cook for about 90 seconds, flipping after every 15 seconds.
15. With a slotted spoon, transfer the doughnuts onto a paper towel-lined plate to drain.
16. Coat the warm doughnuts with powdered sugar and enjoy.

Nutritional Information:

Calories 77.5; Fat 2.3g; Cholesterol 0.0mg; Sodium 122.7mg; Carbohydrates 12.8g; Protein 2.3g

6. EASY-TO-MAKE CHOCO DOUGHNUTS

Preparation Time: 3 minutes
Cooking Time: 12 minutes
Servings: 12

Ingredients:

- ¼ tsp baking soda
- ¼ cup coconut flour
- 3 tbsp cocoa powder
- ¼ cup melted butter

- Two large eggs
- ¼ tsp sea salt
- ¼ cup Stevia
- 1/3 cup Powdered Sugar

Directions:

1. Keep the oven ready by preheating at 350 degrees and coat the Doughnut pan with cooking spray.
2. Mix the dry and wet ingredients in separate bowls and then blend them to make the batter.
3. Pour the batter into the doughnut pan and bake them for 10 minutes. Put on a wire rack to cool down and then serve.

Nutritional Information:

Protein: 0.9g; Fat: 11g; Carbohydrate: 2.3g

7. PEANUT DELIGHT WITH CHOCOLATE TOPPING

Preparation Time: 3 minutes
Cooking Time: 30 minutes
Servings: 12

Ingredients for making peanut Doughnuts:

- 1 tsp stevia glycerite
- 2 cups peanut flour
- 1 tsp baking powder
- 1/8 tsp baking soda
- 1 tsp vanilla extract
- Three eggs
- ½ cup Stevia
- 1 tsp sea salt
- 1¼ cups almond milk

Ingredients for making chocolate topping:

- ¼ cup Stevia
- ¼ cup butter
- ½ tsp vanilla extract
- ¼ cup almond milk (vanilla flavored)
- 6 tbsp cocoa powder

Directions:

1. Keep the oven ready by preheating at 350 degrees and line the Doughnut pan with paper liners.
2. Put all the Doughnut-making ingredients in a mixing bowl and use a hand blender to make the smooth batter.
3. Pour the batter into the Doughnut pan and bake them for 25 minutes. Keep them on a wire rack to cool down.
4. To make the frosting, you will have to melt the butter and add the other ingredients.
5. Spread this mixture over the Doughnuts and let them rest for a few minutes so that the chocolate coating can set.

Nutritional Information:

Protein: 12g; Fat: 8.7g; Carbohydrate: 7.9g

8. CHOCO PUMPKIN MAGIC BLAST

Preparation Time: 5 minutes
Cooking Time: 30 minutes
Servings: 24

Ingredients:

- 8 oz canned pumpkin
- 1 tsp vanilla extract
- One egg
- 1 tsp baking soda
- 8 oz peanut butter
- 4 oz melted butter
- 2 tbsp cocoa powder
- 1 cup Stevia

Directions:

1. Keep the oven ready by preheating it at 350 degrees.
2. Measure necessary amounts of ingredients in a bowl and then use a hand blender to make smooth Doughnut batter.
3. Pour the batter into a lined Doughnut pan and bake them for 25 minutes. Allow cooling down for 5 minutes and then serve.

Nutritional Information:

Protein: 3g; Fat: 5g; Carbohydrate: 2g

9. CARIBBEAN COCOA DOUGHNUTS

Preparation Time: 40 minutes
Cooking Time: 1 hour 10 minutes
Servings: 12

Ingredients:

- 3 tbsp cooking oil
- 1 C. granulated sugar
- Two eggs
- 1 C. milk
- 1 tsp vanilla
- 3 3/4 C. almond milk
- 4 tsp baking powder
- 1/2 tsp salt
- 1/3 C. cocoa

Directions:

1. In a bowl, add 3 tbsp of the oil, milk, eggs, sugar, and vanilla and mix well.
2. Add the flour, cocoa powder, baking powder, and salt and mix until well combined.
3. With a doughnut cutter, cut the doughnuts.
4. Then, with the cap of a bottle, cut a hole in the center of each doughnut.
5. In a deep skillet, add the oil and cook until its temperature reaches 375 degrees F.
6. Add the doughnuts in batches and cook until golden brown from both sides.
7. Add the doughnuts in batches and cook for about 2-4 minutes, flipping once halfway through.
8. With a slotted spoon, transfer the doughnuts onto a paper towel-lined plate to drain.
9. Enjoy.

Nutritional Information:

Calories 272.6; Fat5.5g; Cholesterol 38.1mg; Sodium 240.3mg; Carbohydrates 49.2g; Protein 6.2g

CHAPTER 2: GLAZED DOUGHNUT RECIPES

1. HOW TO MAKE DONUT GLAZE

Preparation Time: 5 minutes
Cooking Time: 7 minutes
Servings: 1

Ingredients:

- 1/4 C. whole milk
- 1 tsp almond extract
- 1 tsp vanilla extract
- 2 C. confectioners' sugar, sifted

Directions:

1. In a pan, add the milk and vanilla over low heat and cook until warm.
2. Add the sifted confectioners' sugar and beat until well combined.
3. Remove the glaze from the heat and arrange it over a bowl of warm water.
4. Coat your doughnuts with the glaze and enjoy!

Nutritional Information:

Calories 39.7; Fat 0.0g; Cholesterol 0.2mg; Sodium 1.1mg; Carbohydrates 9.7g; Protein 0.0g

2. ORANGE GLAZED VEGGIE PUFFS

Preparation Time: 15 minutes
Cooking Time: 35 minutes
Servings: 8

Ingredients

- Vegetable oil
- Two eggs
- 1/2 C. brown sugar
- 1/2 C. white sugar
- 2 tbsp butter, melted
- 1/2 C. milk
- 2 tbsp cooking sherry
- 1 tsp vanilla
- 1 1/2 tsp orange zest
- 1 C. zucchini, shredded drained
- 3 1/2 C. flour
- 1 tbsp baking powder
- 3/4 tsp salt
- 1 tsp cinnamon
- 1/2 tsp nutmeg
- Topping
- 2 C. powdered sugar
- 3 tbsp orange juice

Directions:

1. In a bowl, add the flour, baking powder, cinnamon, nutmeg, and salt and mix well.
2. In another bowl, add the eggs and beat well.
3. Add the cream and both sugars and beat until creamy.
4. Add the sherry, milk, melted butter, vanilla, and orange zest and beat until well combined.
5. Add the zucchini and stir to combine.
6. Add the flour mixture and mix until just combined.
7. In a deep skillet, add the oil and cook until its temperature reaches 370 degrees F.
8. With a tsp, add the mixture and cook until golden brown from both sides.
9. With a slotted spoon, transfer the doughnuts onto a paper towel-lined plate to drain.
10. For the glaze: in a bowl, add the powdered sugar and orange juice and beat until well combined.
11. Coat the warm doughnuts with the glaze and enjoy.

Nutritional Information:

Calories 478.9; Fat 5.2g; Cholesterol 56.2mg; Sodium 411.8mg; Carbohydrates 100.4g; Protein 8.0g

3. GLAZED HARVEST DONUTS

Preparation Time: 10 minutes
Cooking Time: 20 minutes
Servings: 12

Ingredients:

- 1 1/4 oz. yeast, package
- 1/4 C. warm water
- 1/2 C. of lukewarm milk
- 1/4 C. lukewarm buttermilk
- 1/2 tsp salt
- 3 tbsp melted butter
- 1/4 C. sugar
- 2 1/2 C. gluten-free flour
- One egg
- Four drops of essential lemon oil, optional
- Four drops of essential lavender oil, optional
- 3/4 C. of lukewarm milk
- Glaze Ingredients
- 1/2 C. powdered sugar
- 3 tbsp blueberries
- 1/2 tsp vanilla
- 1 -2 tsp milk

Directions:

1. Set your oven to 425 degrees F before doing anything else, and lightly grease a doughnut pan.
2. In a bowl, add the warm water and yeast and mix well.
3. Add the butter, buttermilk, 1/2 C. of the milk, eggs, flour, sugar, and salt and beat until well combined.
4. With plastic wrap, cover the bowl and keep aside for about 50-60 minutes.
5. Add 3/4 C. of the milk and mix until a dough forms.
6. In the prepared doughnut holes, place the mixture evenly.
7. Cook in the oven for about 7-10 minutes.
8. Meanwhile, for the glaze: in a food processor, add all the ingredients and pulse until smooth.
9. Carefully remove the doughnuts from the pan and keep them aside to cool.
10. Coat the cooled doughnuts with the glaze and enjoy.

Nutritional Information:

Calories 96.9; Fat 4.5g; Cholesterol 26.9mg; Sodium 148.0mg; Carbohydrates 12.2g; Protein 2.7g

4. GLAZED WITH IRISH CREAM DONUTS

Preparation Time: 5 minutes
Cooking Time: 25 minutes
Servings: 12

Ingredients:

- ½ tsp baking soda
- 1½ tsp baking powder
- 2 cups wheat flour
- ½ tsp slat
- 2/3 cup cocoa powder
- 1/3 cup granulated Stevia
- ¼ cup melted butter
- Three eggs, lightly beaten
- 20 drops of vanilla-flavored stevia
- ½ cup almond milk
- ½ tsp cornstarch
- Ingredients for Irish cream glaze:
- 3 tbsp Irish cream liqueur
- 3 tbsp almond milk
- ½ cup powdered Stevia

Directions:

1. Keep the oven ready by preheating at 325 degrees and grease the donut pans with cooking spray.
2. Whisk the cocoa powder with wheat flour, Stevia, baking soda, baking powder, cornstarch, and salt, and then blend in the eggs, vanilla, butter, stevia almond milk at the end. This will make a smooth batter.
3. Pour the batter into the greased donut pan and bake them for 20 minutes. Keep the donuts on a wire rack to allow cooling.
4. Make the glaze by mixing all the ingredients in a bowl and then drizzle the mixture on the donuts. Let the glaze set and then serve.

Nutritional Information:

Protein: 1.2g; Fat: 7g; Carbohydrate: 5g

5. PUMPKIN MAGIC DONUTS WITH SWEET GLAZE

Preparation Time: 7 minutes
Cooking Time: 27 minutes
Servings: 7

Ingredients:

- 1.5 tsp baking powder
- ½ tsp salt
- 1½ cup peanut flour
- 1/8 tsp ground cloves
- 1 tsp ground cinnamon
- 2 tbsp coconut oil
- Three eggs
- 1 cup canned pumpkin
- ½ tsp ground nutmeg
- ¼ tsp ground ginger
- 2 tbsp almond milk (unsweetened)
- ½ cup Stevia
- Ingredients for the glaze:
- ¼ tsp vanilla extract
- ¼ cup powdered Stevia
- Two drops of stevia glycerite
- 1 tbsp almond milk

Directions:

1. Mix the wet and dry ingredients in separate bowls and then blend them to make the donut batter.
2. Pour them in a greased donut pan and then bake for 25 minutes at 350 degrees.
3. While the donuts are being baked, make the sweet coating by mixing all the ingredients.
4. Allow the donuts to cool down a bit, and then coat them with the glaze mixture. Let the coating harden up before serving.

Nutritional Information:

Protein: 3g; Fat: 2.9g; Carbohydrate: 5.5g

6. ORANGE GLAZED VEGGIE DONUTS

Preparation Time: 1 hours
Cooking Time: 2 hours

Ingredients

- 4 tbsp of melted butter
- 2 C. white sugar
- 1/2 tsp cinnamon
- 2 eggs
- 7 -8 C. flour
- 2 C. milk
- 2 tbsp sugar
- 2 tsp cream of tartar
- 2 tbsp oil
- 1 tsp baking soda
- 4 tsp baking powder
- 1/2 tsp salt
- 1/2 tsp nutmeg

Directions

1. In a bowl, add the flour, baking soda, baking powder, cream of tartar, nutmeg, cinnamon and salt and mix well.
2. Now, sift the flour mixture into another bowl.
3. In another bowl, add the eggs, sugar and butter and beat until creamy.
4. Add the flour mixture, alternating with the milk and mix until well combined.
5. Place the dough onto a floured surface and roll into 1/4-inch thickness.
6. With a doughnut cutter, cut the doughnuts.
7. In a deep skillet, add the oil and cook until its temperature reaches to 365 degrees F.
8. Add the doughnuts in batches and cook until golden brown from both sides.
9. With a slotted spoon, transfer the doughnuts onto a paper towel-lined plate to drain.
10. Coat the warm doughnuts with the sugar and enjoy.

Nutritional Information:

Calories 80.6; Fat 1.2g; Cholesterol 8.7mg; Sodium 65.7mg; Carbohydrates 15.7g; Protein 1.7g

CHAPTER 3: FRUIT BAKED DOUGHNUT RECIPES

1. APPLE RAISIN DONUTS

Preparation Time: 2 hrs.
Cooking Time: 2 hrs. 5 minutes
Servings: 20

Ingredients:

- 7 g dry yeast
- 1 C. Reduced-fat milk
- 2 1/4 C. flour
- 2 tsp salt
- One egg, beaten
- 1 1/2 C. raisins
- One apple, peeled, cored, and chopped
- oil
- powdered sugar

Directions:

1. In a bowl, place 1/4 C. of the milk and sprinkle with the yeast.
2. Keep aside for about 5 minutes.
3. In another bowl, add the flour and salt and mix well.
4. Add the egg and remaining milk and beat until well combined.
5. Add the yeast mixture, apple, and raisins and mix until well combined.
6. Keep aside in a warm area until doubled in bulk.
7. With two metal spoons, make the balls from the mixture.

8. In a deep skillet, add the oil and cook until its temperature reaches 325 degrees F.

9. Add the doughnuts in batches and cook for about 8 minutes, flipping frequently.

10. With a slotted spoon, transfer the doughnuts onto a paper towel-lined plate to drain.

11. Coat the doughnuts with powdered sugar and keep them aside to cool.

12. After cooling, coat with the powdered sugar and enjoy.

Nutritional Information:

Calories 100.9; Fat 0.9g; Cholesterol 11.0mg; Sodium 243.8mg; Carbohydrates 21.3g; Protein 2.6g

2. MOM'S EASY APPLE DONUTS

Preparation Time: 5 minutes
Cooking Time: 20 minutes
Servings: 3

Ingredients:

- 3 tbsp butter, softened
- 3/4 C. sugar
- Three eggs
- 1 C. applesauce
- 1 tsp vanilla extract
- 4 1/2 C. almond milk
- 3 1/2 tsp baking powder
- 1 tsp salt
- 1/2-3/4 tsp cinnamon, ground
- 1/4-1/2 tsp nutmeg, ground
- 1/4 C. milk
- oil
- sugar

Directions:

1. In a bowl, add the flour, baking powder, cinnamon, nutmeg, and salt and mix well.
2. In another bowl, add the sugar and butter and beat until creamy.
3. Add the eggs, one at a time, and beat well.

4. Add the vanilla extract and applesauce and beat until well combined.
5. Add the flour mixture, alternating with the milk, and mix until a thick mixture is formed.
6. In a deep skillet, add the oil and cook until its temperature reaches 375 degrees F.
7. With a tsp, place the mixture and cook until golden brown from both sides.
8. With a slotted spoon, transfer the doughnuts onto a paper towel-lined plate to drain.
9. Coat the warm doughnuts with the sugar and enjoy.

Nutritional Information:

Calories 121.6; Fat 2.0g; Cholesterol 23.5mg; Sodium 151.0mg; Carbohydrates 22.8g; Protein 2.8g

3. FANTASTIC APPLE DONUTS WITH APPLE GLAZE

Preparation Time: 5 minutes
Cooking Time: 1 hour 20 minutes
Servings: 12

Ingredients:

- 1 tbsp baking powder
- 1 tbsp cinnamon
- 3 cups blanched wheat flour
- Four eggs
- 1 tsp sea salt
- ¼ tsp nutmeg
- ½ cup butter
- 2 cups powdered sugar
- 2 tsp apple extract
- 1 cup brewed apple tea
- Ingredients for making the glaze:
- ½ cup of coconut oil
- ½ cup powdered Stevia
- 1 tsp apple extract

Directions:

1. Keep the oven ready by preheating at 350 degrees and grease the donut pan with cooking spray.
2. Put the wheat flour in a bowl and mix the baking powder, cinnamon, salt, and nutmeg with it. Keep this mixture aside.
3. Put the sweetener, apple tea, eggs, and vanilla extract in a blender and beat to make a smooth paste. Add the flour mixture to this paste and make the donut batter.
4. Pour the batter into a donut pan and bake for an hour.
5. To make the glaze, you will have to mix all the ingredients in a small pan over low heat, ensuring the sweetener is dissolved correctly.
6. Let the donuts cool down, and then add the spread the glaze on top.

Nutritional Information:

Protein: 5g; Fat: 22g; Carbohydrate: 6.7g

4. APPLE DONUTS

Preparation Time: 5 Minutes
Cooking Time: 20 Minutes

Ingredients

- 3 tbsp butter, softened
- 3/4 C. sugar
- 1/4-1/2 tsp nutmeg, ground
- 3 eggs
- 1/4 C. milk
- 1 C. applesauce
- 2 tbsp oil
- 1 tsp vanilla extract
- 2 tbsp sugar
- 1/2 C. almond milk
- 1/2 tsp baking powder
- 1 tsp salt
- 1/2-3/4 tsp cinnamon, ground

Directions

1. In a bowl, add the flour, baking powder, cinnamon, nutmeg and salt and mix well.
2. In another bowl, add the sugar and butter and beat until creamy.
3. Add the eggs, one at a time and beat well.
4. Add the vanilla extract and applesauce and beat until well combined.
5. Add the flour mixture, alternating with the milk and mix until a thick mixture is formed.
6. In a deep skillet, add the oil and cook until its temperature reaches to 375 degrees F.
7. With a tsp, place the mixture and cook until golden brown from both sides.
8. With a slotted spoon, transfer the doughnuts onto a paper towel-lined plate to drain.
9. Coat the warm doughnuts with the sugar and enjoy.

Nutritional Information:

Calories 121.6; Fat 2.0g; Cholesterol 23.5mg; Sodium 151.0mg; Carbohydrates 22.8g; Protein 2.8g

5. BATON ROUGE INSPIRED DONUTS

Preparation Time: 10 minutes
Cooking Time: 35 minutes
Servings: 1

Ingredients:

- 1 1/2 C. sifted flour
- 1 3/4 tsp baking powder
- 1/2 tsp salt
- 1/2 tsp nutmeg
- 1/2 C. sugar
- 1/3 C. shortening

- One beaten egg
- 1/4 C. milk
- 1/2 C. grated apple
- 1/2 C. butter, melted
- cinnamon sugar

Directions:

1. Set your oven to 350 degrees F before doing anything else and grease a doughnut pan.
2. In a bowl, add the flour, sugar, baking powder, nutmeg, and salt and mix well.
3. With a pastry blender, cut in the shortening.
4. Add the milk, egg, and apples and mix well.
5. In the prepared doughnut pan, place the mixture about 2/3 of the full.
6. Cook in the oven for about 20-25 minutes.
7. Coat the warm doughnuts with 1/2 C. of the melted butter and then with the cinnamon-sugar.
8. Enjoy.

Nutritional Information:

Calories 220.1; Fat 14.1g; Cholesterol 38.6mg; Sodium 213.0mg; Carbohydrates 21.4g; Protein 2.4g

6. A HOMESTEADER'S FAVORITE

Preparation Time: 20 minutes
Cooking Time: 32 minutes
Servings: 12

Ingredients:

- 3 tbsp granulated sugar
- 2 1/2 tsp cinnamon, divided
- 2 C. almond milk
- 1 1/2 tsp baking powder
- 1 1/2 tsp baking soda
- 1/4 tsp salt
- Two large egg whites, beaten
- 2/3 C. packed brown sugar
- 1/2 C. apple butter
- 1/3 C. pure maple syrup
- 1/3 C. apple cider
- 1/3 C. nonfat vanilla yogurt
- 3 tbsp canola oil
- 1 tsp vanilla extract

Directions:

1. Set your oven to 400 degrees F before doing anything else and grease the molds of 2 mini bundt cake pans.
2. In a bowl, add the granulated sugar and 1/2 tsp of the cinnamon and mix well.
3. Place some of the cinnamon sugar evenly and shake out the excess in the bottom of the prepared cake molds.
4. In a bowl, add the flour, baking soda, baking powder, remaining 2 tsp of the cinnamon and salt, and mix well.
5. In a second bowl, add the brown sugar, egg whites, yogurt, maple syrup, apple butter, apple cider, canola oil, and vanilla extract and beat until well combined.
6. Add the flour mixture and mix until just combined.
7. In the prepared cake molds, place the mixture evenly and top with the reserved cinnamon sugar.
8. Cook in the oven for about 10-12 minutes.
9. Remove from the oven and keep onto a wire rack to cool for about 2 minutes.
10. Carefully invert the doughnuts onto the wire rack and enjoy.

Nutritional Information:

Calories 214.1; Fat 3.7g; Cholesterol 0.0mg; Sodium 268.1mg; Carbohydrates 42.5g; Protein 2.8g

7. HONEY DELIGHT WITH PISTACHIO BLAST

Preparation Time: 5 minutes
Cooking Time: 20 minutes
Servings: 12

Ingredients:

- ½ cup almond meal
- ½ tsp salt
- ½ cup coconut flour
- One egg
- ¼ cup unsweetened apple sauce
- 1 tsp vanilla extract
- ¼ cup honey
- 1/3 cup almond milk
- ¼ cup roasted and ground pistachio nuts
- 1 tsp baking powder
- 1 tbsp coconut oil
- Ingredients for top coating:
- ¼ cup honey
- ½ cup unsalted pistachio nuts, roasted and ground

Directions:

1. Keep the oven ready by preheating at 350 degrees and coat the mini donut pan with cooking spray.
2. Put the coconut flour in a bowl and other dry ingredients and mix the wet ingredients in another bowl. Now, blend them to make the donut batter.
3. Pour the batter into a donut pan and bake them for 15 minutes.
4. While the donuts are cooling, you can make the topping by mixing the ground with honey and cooking them in the microwave for 20 seconds.
5. When the donuts are ready, spread the topping mixture over them and allow some time to rest before serving.

Nutritional Information:

Protein: 1.2g; Fat: 17g; Carbohydrate: 9.2g

8. BANANA BROWN SUGAR DONUTS

Preparation Time: 15 minutes
Cooking Time: 23 minutes
Servings: 22

Ingredients:

- Two medium bananas
- Two egg whites
- 1 tbsp vegetable oil
- 1 C. packed light brown sugar
- 1 1/2 C. almond milk
- 3/4 C. whole grain wheat flour
- 2 tsp baking powder
- 1/2 tsp baking soda
- 1 tsp vanilla extract
- 1 tbsp sugar
- 1 tsp ground cinnamon

Directions:

1. Set your oven to 425 degrees F before doing anything else and grease a baking sheet.
2. In a bowl, add the oil, egg whites, sugar, and bananas and beat until well combined.
3. Add flours, baking soda, baking powder, cinnamon, and vanilla and mix until well combined.

4. Keep aside for about 5 minutes.
5. With a tbsp, place the dough onto the prepared baking sheet, and with a spatula, press slightly.
6. Then, with the cap of a bottle, cut a hole in the center of each doughnut.
7. Cook in the oven for about 6-10 minutes.
8. Enjoy warm.

Nutritional Information:

Calories 102.7; Fat 0.8g; Cholesterol 0.0mg; Sodium 69.7mg; Carbohydrates 22.5g; Protein 1.8g

9. COCONUT GLAZED BANANA DONUTS

Preparation Time: 10 minutes
Cooking Time: 40 minutes
Servings: 12

Ingredients:

- 3 1/2 C. flour
- 1 1/3 C. sugar
- 2 tsp baking powder
- Two ripe bananas, mashed
- 1 tbsp vanilla
- 1 1/2 C. water
- 1/4 C. crushed pineapple
- 6 C. oil
- cinnamon-sugar mixture
- Syrup
- 1/3 C. water
- 1/3 C. sugar
- 1 C. coconut milk
- 1/8 tsp sea salt
- 1 tsp vanilla

Directions:

1. In a bowl, add the flour, baking powder, and sugar and mix well.
2. Add the pineapple, bananas, water, and vanilla extract and mix until a sticky dough forms.
3. In a deep skillet, add 3-inch deep oil and cook until its temperature reaches 350 degrees F.
4. With a scooper, add the mixture in batches and cook until golden brown from both sides.
5. With a slotted spoon, transfer the doughnuts onto a paper towel-lined plate to drain.
6. Coat the warm doughnuts with cinnamon sugar and enjoy.

Nutritional Information:

Calories 1313.8; Fat 113.4g; Cholesterol 0.0mg; Sodium 96.0mg; Carbohydrates 73.5g; Protein 4.2g

10. DELICIOUS BANANA FLAVORED DONUTS

Preparation Time: 3 minutes
Cooking Time: 15 minutes
Servings: 4

Ingredients:

- ¼ cup mashed banana
- ½ tsp baking powder
- 2 tbsp coconut flour
- A pinch of salt
- One packet of stevia
- Two egg whites
- A pinch of cinnamon

Directions:

1. Keep the oven ready by preheating at 350 degrees and grease the donut pan with cooking spray.
2. Put all the ingredients in a bowl and use a hand blender to make a smooth batter.
3. You will have to reserve a bit of batter to make the coating on the cooked donuts.
4. Pour the batter into the donut pan and bake them for 13 minutes and then allow cooling down.
5. Spread the batter as the coating and then serve.

Nutritional Information:

Protein: 1.6g; Fat: 2.5g; Carbohydrate: 10.2g

11. PROTEIN BOOSTER BANANA FLAVORED DONUTS

Preparation Time: 5 minutes
Cooking Time: 13 minutes
Servings: 12

Ingredients:

- One banana, mashed
- 1/3 liquid egg white
- 2 tbsp coconut flour
- 4 tbsp protein powder
- ½ tsp ground cinnamon
- 1 tsp baking soda
- 2 tsp liquid stevia
- 2 tbsp almond milk
- 1 tbsp powdered Stevia

Directions:

1. You will have to use two separate bowls to blend the dry and wet ingredients and then mix them to make the donuts batter.
2. Pour the batter into a greased donut pan and bake them for 11 minutes at 350 degrees.
3. Allow the donuts to cool down and then serve.

Nutritional Information:

Protein: 2g; Fat: 0.6g; Carbohydrate: 1.7g

12. STRAWBERRY JELLY DONUTS

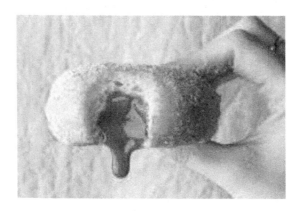

Preparation Time: 1 hour
Cooking Time: 1 hour 4 minutes
Servings: 40

Ingredients:

- 2 (1/4 oz.) envelope dry yeast
- 1/4 C. warm water
- 1 1/2 C. lukewarm milk
- 3/4 C. sugar
- 1 tsp salt
- Two eggs
- 6 tbsp shortening
- 5 C. flour
- oil
- 1 (13 1/2 oz.) jar strawberry jelly
- confectioners' sugar

Directions:

1. In a bowl, add the warm water and sprinkle with the yeast.
2. Keep aside for about minutes.
3. In a bowl, add the 2 C. of the flour, yeast mixture, sugar, salt, milk, shortening, sugar, eggs, and an electric mixer; beat on low speed until well combined.
4. Add the remaining flour, 1/2 C. at a time, and mix until a non-sticky dough forms.
5. With your hands, knead until smooth and elastic dough forms.
6. In a greased bowl, place the dough.

7. With plastic wrap, cover the dough and keep it in a warm place for about 1 hour.

8. Place the dough onto a floured surface and roll into 1/2-inch thickness.

9. With a doughnut cutter, cut the doughnuts.

10. Keep aside until doubled in size.

11. In a deep skillet, add 4 C. of the oil and cook until its temperature reaches 350 degrees F.

12. Add the doughnuts in batches and cook until golden brown from both sides.

13. Add the doughnuts in batches and cook for about 2-4 minutes, flipping once halfway through.

14. With a slotted spoon, transfer the doughnuts onto a paper towel-lined plate to drain.

15. With a pastry injector, fill each doughnut with the jelly evenly.

16. Coat with the confectioners' sugar and enjoy.

Nutritional Information:

Calories 124.0; Fat 2.6g; Cholesterol 10.5mg; Sodium 69.5mg; Carbohydrates 22.8g; Protein 2.3g

CHAPTER 4: PROTEIN POWDER BAKED DOUGHNUT RECIPES

1. BACON BLAST WITH MAPLE FLAVOR TOPPING

Preparation Time: 5 minutes
Cooking Time: 35 minutes
Servings: 12

Ingredients:

- ¼ cup coconut flour
- Cups wheat flour
- ½ cup butter
- 2 Egg white
- ½ tsp salt
- Two eggs
- ¼ tsp stevia extract
- 1 tsp maple extract
- 2 tsp baking powder
- ½ tsp cornstarch
- ½ cup Stevia
- ½ cup almond milk

Ingredients for bacon topping:

- ¾ tsp maple extract
- Eight slices of bacon, cooked to make crisp and then chopped
- ¾ cups powdered Stevia
- 3 tbsp almond milk

Directions:

1. Keep the oven ready by preheating at 325 degrees and grease the donut pan with cooking spray.
2. Keep the almond milk aside, and then mix the wet and dry ingredients in separate bowls. Now blend the two mixtures, slowly adding the almond milk in portions. Make the batter smooth by using a hand blender.
3. Pour the batter into a donut pan and bake them for 18 minutes, making sure that the edges are golden brown.
4. Make the topping by mixing the sweetener with almond milk and maple extract.
5. Top the donuts with this glaze mixture, and then sprinkle the chopped crisp bacon pieces over them. Let the donuts stand for 15 minutes so that the bacon pieces stick with them appropriately.

Nutritional Information:

Protein: 7g; Fat: 19g; Carbohydrate: 6g

2. BROWN BUTTER COATED DONUTS WITH CINNAMON TWIST

Preparation Time: 7 minutes
Cooking Time: 25 minutes
Servings: 8

Ingredients:

- 1 tsp ground cinnamon
  - cups wheat flour
- 2 tbsp vanilla-flavored whey protein powder
- ¼ cup granulated Stevia
- 10 drops liquid stevia
- 1.5 tsp baking powder
- Two eggs, lightly beaten
- ¼ tsp salt
- 3 tbsp melted butter
- ¼ tsp vanilla extract
- ¼ cup almond milk
- Ingredients for making browned butter coating:
- 2 tbsp heavy cream
- 3 tbsp butter
- 7 tbsp powdered Stevia
- ¼ tsp vanilla extract

Directions:

1. Keep the oven ready by preheating it at 325 degrees and coat the donut pan with cooking spray.
2. Put the dry ingredients in a bowl and then add the wet ingredients one by one to make a smooth batter.
3. Pour the batter into the donut pan, bake them for 18 minutes and then allow cooling down in a wire rack.
4. To make the butter coating, heat the butter in a saucepan till it turns brown and fragrant, and then adds the other frosting ingredients to it.
5. Coat the donuts with this mixture and allow some resting time before serving.

Nutritional Information:

Protein: 2g; Fat: 13g; Carbohydrate: 3.2g

3. GINGERY DONUTS WITH LEMON TWIST

Preparation Time: 5 minutes
Cooking Time: 15 minutes
Servings: 12

Ingredients:

- 2 tsp ground cinnamon
- ¾ cup almond meal
- 2 tsp ground ginger
- 1/3 cup coconut oil
- Two packets of protein powder
- Two tsp of Vanilla Essense
- ¼ tsp ground cloves
- 3 tbsp molasses
- 1 tsp vanilla extract
- 1 cup baking blend (gluten-free)
- ½ tsp salt
- 1/3 tsp baking soda
- 1 tbsp stevia powder
- Three eggs

Ingredients for making lemon glaze:

- 2 tsp fresh lemon juice
- 2 tbsp coconut milk
- 1 tbsp stevia powder
- 1 tbsp protein powder
- 1 tsp of Vanilla Essence
- 2 tbsp lemon zest
- 1 tbsp coconut butter

Directions:

1. Keep the oven ready by preheating it at 350 degrees and coat the donut pan with cooking spray.
2. Mix the dry and wet ingredients in two bowls and then blend them to make the donut batter.
3. Pour the batter into the donut pan and bake them for 12 minutes.
4. While the donuts are being baked, make the lemon glaze by mixing all the ingredients thoroughly and drizzle it over the donuts. Let the coating set for some time and then serve.

Nutritional Information:

Protein: 2.6g; Fat: 13g; Carbohydrate: 8.2g

4. GINGER-BREAD-MAN WITH VANILLA FANTASY

Preparation Time: 6 minutes
Cooking Time: 20 minutes
Servings: 12

Ingredients:

- ¼ cup Stevia
- tsp ground cinnamon
- 2 cups wheat flour
- ¼ tsp salt
- ¼ cup whey protein powder
- 2 tsp baking powder
- 2 tsp ground ginger
- ¼ tsp ground cloves
- 2 oz cream cheese
- Two eggs
- 2 tsp molasses
- 2 tbsp coconut oil
- 1/3 cup almond milk
- ¼ tsp liquid stevia extract

Ingredients for making vanilla frosting:

- ¼ cup almond milk
- 4 oz cream cheese
- 1 tsp vanilla extract
- 6 tbsp powdered Stevia
- Seeds of one vanilla bean

Directions:

1. Keep the oven ready by preheating at 325 degrees and coat the donut pan with cooking spray.
2. Put the dry and wet ingredients in separate bowls and then blend them to make the donut batter. Pour the batter into the donut pan and bake them for 15 minutes. Allow the donuts to cool down in wire racks.
3. Make the vanilla frosting by blending all the ingredients and then spread the mixture over the donuts. Let them stand for some time and then serve.

Nutritional Information:

Protein: 8g; Fat: 18g; Carbohydrate: 6g

5. COCONUT MAGIC COATED DONUTS WITH CHOCOLATE TWIST

Preparation Time: 5 minutes
Cooking Time: 25 minutes
Servings: 14

Ingredients:

- tsp baking powder
- ½ cup coconut flour
- 6 tbsp Stevia
- ¼ tsp salt
- ½ tsp vanilla extract
- ¼ cup melted coconut oil
- ½ cup of coconut milk
- Five eggs
- 2 tbsp vanilla-flavored whey protein powder

Ingredients for making top coating:

- 3 tbsp butter
- ¾ cup shredded coconut
- 1/3 cup whipping cream
- ¼ tsp cornstarch
- 1 tbsp coconut sugar
- 5 tbsp powdered Stevia
- A pinch of salt
- Ingredients for making chocolate drizzle:
- ½ cup of chocolate chips (unsweetened)
- ½ tbsp coconut oil

Directions:

1. Keep the oven ready by preheating at 325 degrees and coat the donut pan with coconut oil.
2. Mix the dry and wet ingredients in separate bowls and then blend them to make the donut batter. Make sure that the batter is smooth by using a hand blender.
3. Pour the batter into a donut pan and bake them for 15 minutes, ensuring that they become golden brown.
4. To make the topping, the shredded coconut is toasted till golden brown, then mix the butter and all other ingredients in a saucepan over medium heat. Add the shredded coconut and cook for a few minutes, making sure that they do not burn. This coconut caramel mixture is to be spread over the donuts and then allow resting to set the coating.
5. Mix the chocolate chips with the coconut oil and then drizzle the mixture over the coconut coated donuts.

Nutritional Information:

Protein: 5.7g; Fat: 19g; Carbohydrate: 5.4g

CHAPTER 5: BUTTERY BAKED DOUGHNUT RECIPES

1. CREAMY-BUTTERY FROSTED DONUTS

Preparation Time: 5 minutes
Cooking Time: 25 minutes
Servings: 6

Ingredients:

- 2 tsp cinnamon
- Cup wheat flour
- Two large eggs
- 1 tbsp coconut flour
- 2 tbsp water
- ½ cup pumpkin puree
- ¼ tsp vanilla extract
- ½ cup granulated Stevia
- ¼ tsp sea salt
- 1½ tsp baking powder
- Ingredients for making butter-cream frosting:
- ½ cup granulated Stevia
- ¼ tsp vanilla extract
- 3 tbsp butter
- 1 tbsp almond milk

Directions:

1. Keep the oven ready by preheating it at 325 degrees and grease the donut pan with coconut oil.
2. Mix the dry and wet ingredients in two bowls and then blend them to make the donut batter.
3. Pour the batter into the greased donut pan and bake for 15 minutes.
4. While the donuts are being baked, make use of the time to make the frosting. Use a hand blender to mix all the frosting ingredients and keep it in a piping bag.
5. When the donuts are cooked and cooled down a bit, but the frosting over them to serve.

Nutritional Information:

Protein: 2.6g; Fat: 23g; Carbohydrate: 3.2g

2. SWEET BUTTERMILK DONUT

Preparation Time: 30 minutes
Cooking Time: 40 minutes
Servings: 16

Ingredients:

- Two eggs, beaten
- 2 C. buttermilk
- 1/4 C. butter, melted
- 5 C. All-purpose flour
- 1 C. sugar
- 1 tsp nutmeg
- 1/2 tsp cinnamon
- 2 tsp baking soda
- 1 tsp baking powder
- 2 tsp salt
- 2 tsp cornstarch
- 1/2 C. sugar, set aside in a bowl

Directions:

1. In a bowl, add the flour mix, sugar, baking soda, baking powder, cornstarch, spices, and salt and mix well.
2. In another bowl, add the butter, eggs, and buttermilk and beat until well combined.
3. Add the flour mixture and gently stir until just combined.
4. Now, with your hands, knead until a dough forms.
5. Keep aside for about 15 minutes.
6. Place the dough onto a floured surface and roll into 1/3-1/2-inch thickness.
7. With a doughnut cutter, cut the doughnuts.
8. Then, with the cap of a bottle, cut a hole in the center of each doughnut.
9. In a deep skillet, add 2-3-inch of the canola oil and cook until its temperature reaches 375 degrees F.
10. Add the doughnuts in batches and cook until golden brown from both sides.
11. Coat the warm doughnuts with the sugar and enjoy.

Nutritional Information:

Calories 120.3; Fat 3.7g; Cholesterol 32.1mg; Sodium 537.2mg; Carbohydrates 20.4g; Protein 1.8g

3. PEANUT BUTTER DONUTS

Preparation Time: 20 minutes
Cooking Time: 35 minutes
Servings: 8

Ingredients:

- 8 oz. refrigerated crescent dinner rolls
- Filling
- 1/2 C. brown sugar
- 1/2 C. walnuts
- 2 tbsp butter, softened
- 1/2 tsp cinnamon
- 4 tbsp semi-sweet chocolate chips
- 2 tbsp peanut butter
- 3 tbsp peanut butter chips
- 1/2 C. pie filling, mashed

Glaze

- 1/2 C. powdered sugar
- 2 1/2 tsp brewed coffee

Directions:

1. Set your oven to 350 degrees F before doing anything else, and line a baking sheet with a piece of foil.
2. For the filling: in a bowl, add all the ingredients and mix well.
3. Unroll the dough and then carefully divide into crescents.
4. Place the filling onto the wide ends of the crescents, leaving about 1-inch edges.
5. Roll each crescent over the filling into a half-moon shape.
6. In the bottom of the prepared baking sheet, arrange the, arrange the about 1-inch apart.
7. Cook in the oven for about 15 minutes.
8. Remove from the oven and keep onto the wire rack to cool in the pan for about 10 minutes.
9. Meanwhile, for the frosting: in a bowl, add the powdered sugar and coffee and beat until well combined.
10. Drizzle the warm doughnuts with the frosting and enjoy.

Nutritional Information:

Calories 310.8; Fat 14.2g; Cholesterol 21.8mg; Sodium 209.1mg; Carbohydrates 42.6g; Protein 5.7g

4. BUTTERMILK DONUT

Preparation Time: 30 Minutes
Cooking Time: 40 Minutes

Ingredients

- 2 eggs, beaten
- 2 tsp baking soda
- 2 C. buttermilk
- 1 tsp baking powder
- 1/4 C. butter, melted
- 2 tsp salt
- 5 C. gluten-free All-purpose flour mix
- 2 tsp cornstarch
- 1 C. sugar
- 1/2 C. sugar, set aside in a bowl
- 1 tsp nutmeg
- 1/2 tsp cinnamon

Directions

1. In a bowl, add the flour mix, sugar, baking soda, baking powder, cornstarch, spices and salt and mix well.
2. In another bowl, add the butter, eggs and buttermilk and beat until well combined.
3. Add the flour mixture and gently, stir until just combined.
4. Now, with your hands, knead until a dough forms.
5. Keep aside for about 15 minutes.
6. Place the dough onto a floured surface and roll into 1/3-1/2-inch thickness.
7. With a doughnut cutter, cut the doughnuts.
8. Then, with the cap of a bottle, cut a hole in the center of each doughnut.
9. In a deep skillet, add 2-3-inch of the canola oil and cook until its temperature reaches to 375 degrees F.
10. Add the doughnuts in batches and cook until golden brown from both sides.
11. Coat the warm doughnuts with the sugar and enjoy.

Nutritional Information:

Calories 120.3; Fat 3.7g; Cholesterol 32.1mg; Sodium 537.2mg; Carbohydrates 20.4g; Protein 1.8g

5. SWEET BUTTERMILK DONUT: (GLUTEN FREE)

Preparation Time: 3 hours
Cooking Time: 3 hours 30 Minutes

Ingredients

- 2 C. scalded milk
- 1/2 C. butter
- 7 C. sifted flour
- 2/3 C. sugar, divided

Coating

- 1 tsp salt
- 3 C. powdered sugar
- 2 tbsp yeast
- 1/2 tsp salt
- 4 eggs, beaten
- 1/2 tsp vanilla
- 1/4 tsp nutmeg
- 1/2 C. cold water

Directions

1. For the glaze: in a bowl, add all the ingredients and mix until well combined.
2. Keep aside.
3. In a pan, add the hot milk and butter and mix until butter is melted completely.
4. Add 1 tsp of the sugar and salt and mix well.
5. Keep aside to cool.
6. After cooling, add the eggs, remaining sugar, 3 C. of the flour, yeast and nutmeg and mix until well combined.
7. Add the remaining flour and mix until a sticky dough forms.
8. Now, with your hands, knead for about 5 minutes.
9. Keep aside for about 1-1 1/2 hours.
10. 1Place the dough onto a floured surface and roll into desired thickness.
11. 1Cut the dough into desired sized shapes.
12. Keep aside for about 30-45 minutes.
13. In a deep skillet, add the oil and cook until its temperature reaches to 365 degrees F.
14. Add the doughnuts in batches and cook for about 2-4 minutes, flipping once halfway
15. With a slotted spoon, transfer the doughnuts onto a paper towel-lined plate to drain.
16. 1Coat the warm doughnuts with the glaze and enjoy.

Nutritional Information:

Calories 137.5; Fat 2.9g; Cholesterol 22.0mg; Sodium 101.3mg; Carbohydrates 24.8g; Protein 2.9g

CHAPTER 6: BAKED DOUGHNUT WITH FROSTING RECIPES

1. GLAZED VEGGIE DONUTS

Preparation Time: 15 Minutes
Cooking Time: 35 Minutes

Ingredients

- Vegetable oil
- 1 C. zucchini, shredded and drained
- 2 eggs
- 1/2 C. flour
- 1/2 C. brown sugar
- 1 tbsp baking powder
- 1/2 C. white sugar
- 3/4 tsp salt
- 2 tbsp butter, melted
- 1 tsp cinnamon
- 1/2 C. milk
- 1/2 tsp nutmeg
- 2 tbsp cooking sherry

Topping

- 1 tsp vanilla
- 2 C. powdered sugar
- 1/2 tsp orange zest
- 3 tbsp orange juice

Directions

1. In a bowl, add the flour, baking powder, cinnamon, nutmeg and salt and mix well.
2. In another bowl, add the eggs and beat well.
3. Add the cream and both sugars and beat until creamy.
4. Add the sherry, milk, melted butter, vanilla and orange zest and beat until well combined.
5. Add the zucchini and stir to combine.
6. Add the flour mixture and mix until just combined.
7. In a deep skillet, add the oil and cook until its temperature reaches to 370 degrees F.
8. With a tsp, add the mixture and cook until golden brown from both sides.
9. With a slotted spoon, transfer the doughnuts onto a paper towel-lined plate to drain.
10. 1For the glaze: in a bowl, add the powdered sugar and orange juice and beat until well combined.
11. Coat the warm doughnuts with the glaze and enjoy.

Nutritional Information:

Calories 478.9; Fat 5.2g; Cholesterol 56.2mg; Sodium 411.8mg; Carbohydrates 100.4g; Protein 8.0g

2. FROSTED DOUGHNUT

Preparation Time: 10 Minutes
Cooking Time: 35 Minutes

Ingredients

- 1 3/4 C. flour
- 1 egg, beaten
- 1 1/2 tsp baking powder
- 3/4 C. low-fat milk
- 1/2 tsp salt
- jam
- 1/2 tsp ground nutmeg
- Coating
- 1/4 tsp ground cinnamon
- 1/4 C. butter, melted
- 3/4 C. sugar
- 1/3 C. sugar
- 1/3 C. vegetable oil
- 1 tsp ground cinnamon

Directions

1. Set your oven to 350 degrees F before doing anything else and grease a muffin pan.
2. In a bowl, add the flour, baking powder, cinnamon, nutmeg and salt and mix well.
3. In another bowl, add the milk, oil, sugar and egg and beat until well combined.
4. Add the flour mixture and mix until just combined.
5. In the prepared muffin cups, place the mixture about 1/2 full and top each with 1 tsp of the jam.
6. Now, place the remaining mixture over the jam in each muffin cup about 3/4 of the full.
7. Cook in the oven for about 20-25 minutes.
8. Remove from the oven and keep onto the wire rack to cool in the pan for about 5 minutes.
9. Carefully, invert the muffins onto the wire rack to cool completely.
10. In a bowl, place the melted butter.
11. In another bowl, add the sugar and cinnamon and mix well.
12. Immediately, dip the tops in butter and coat with the cinnamon sugar.

Nutritional Information:

Calories 284.8; Fat 12.7g; Cholesterol 31.7mg; Sodium 227.1mg; Carbohydrates 39.7g; Protein 3.5g

3. PUMPKIN DONUTS IN FALL

Preparation Time: 10 minutes
Cooking Time: 20 minutes
Servings: 12

Ingredients:

- 2 C. almond milk
- 1/2 C. packed brown sugar
- 1 1/2 tsp baking powder
- 1 1/2 tsp pumpkin pie spice
- 1/2 tsp salt
- 1/4 tsp baking soda
- 1/2 C. canned pumpkin
- Two eggs
- 1/4 C. milk
- 1/4 C. butter, softened

Frosting

- 1 C. powdered sugar, sifted
- 1/4 tsp vanilla
- 4 -5 tsp milk

Directions:

1. Set your oven to 375 degrees F before doing anything else and grease two baking sheets.
2. For the doughnuts: in a bowl, add the flour, baking powder, baking soda, brown sugar, pumpkin pie spice, and salt and mix well.
3. Add the butter, milk, eggs, and pumpkin and beat on low speed until well combined with an electric mixer.
4. A pastry bag, fitted with a large star tip with a 1/2-inch opening, place the pumpkin mixture.
5. pe the mixture in 3-inch circles. At the bottom of each prepared baking sheet
6. Cook in the oven for about 10-12 minutes.
7. Remove from the oven and place the doughnuts onto a wire rack.
8. For the icing: in a bowl, add the powdered sugar and vanilla and mix well.
9. Add enough milk and mix until a glaze-like icing is formed.
10. Coat the top of each doughnut with the icing and enjoy.

Nutritional Information:

Calories 204.4; Fat 5.1g; Cholesterol 42.1mg; Sodium 245.3mg; Carbohydrates 36.3g; Protein 3.6g

4. FROSTED DOUGHNUTS

Preparation Time: 30 minutes
Cooking Time: 40 minutes
Servings: 1

Ingredients:

- 1 C. milk, lukewarm
- 1 (1/4 oz.) package yeast
- 1 C. lukewarm water
- 1/2 C. shortening
- 2/3 C. sugar
- Two eggs, beaten
- 1 tsp salt
- 7 C. flour

Directions:

1. In a bowl, add the warm water and sprinkle with the yeast.
2. Keep aside for about 10 minutes.
3. Add the milk and stir to combine
4. In another bowl, add sugar and shortening and beat until creamy.
5. Add eggs and beat until well combined.
6. Add the flour and salt, alternating with the milk mixture, and mix until smooth.
7. With plastic wrap, cover the bowl and keep aside in a warm place until doubled in size.
8. Place the dough onto a floured surface and roll into 1/2-inch thickness.

9. With a doughnut cutter, cut the doughnuts.
10. Keep aside until doubled in size.
11. In a deep skillet, add the oil and cook until heated through.
12. Add the doughnuts in batches and cook until golden brown from both sides.
13. With a slotted spoon, transfer the doughnuts onto a paper towel-lined plate to drain.
14. Coat the warm doughnuts with the sugar glaze and enjoy.

Nutritional Information:

Calories 98.5; Fat 2.6g; Cholesterol 8.1mg; Sodium 52.3mg; Carbohydrates 16.3g; Protein 2.2g

5. ONTARIO DONUT SQUARES

Preparation Time: 1 hour
Cooking Time: 1 hour 3 minutes
Servings: 1

Ingredients:

- 2 tbsp yeast
- 1/2 C. warm water
- 6 tbsp margarine
- 1 C. milk, scalding
- 1 C. cold water
- 1 tsp salt
- 1/2 C. sugar
- Three eggs
- 6 -7 C. flour
- Oil

Glaze

- 4 1/2 C. powdered sugar
- 1/2 C. margarine
- 4 tbsp milk
- 2 tbsp maple flavoring

Directions:

1. In a bowl, add 1/2 of the water and sprinkle with the yeast.
2. Keep aside for about 5 minutes.
3. In another bowl, add the hot scalded milk, butter, sugar and salt, and sugar and stir well.
4. Add the cold water and mix until well combined.
5. In the bowl of the mixer, add the yeast mixture and milk mixture.
6. Add flour, 1 C. at a time, and mix until a soft dough forms.
7. Place the dough onto a lightly floured surface and with a rolling pin, roll into a 1/4-1/2 inch thick rectangle.
8. Cut the dough into 2-3x5-6-inch rectangular bars.
9. With a plastic wrap over the bars and keep aside until doubled in size.
10. In a deep skillet, add the oil and cook until its temperature reaches 350 degrees F.
11. Add the doughnut bars in batches and cook until golden brown from both sides.
12. With a slotted spoon, transfer the doughnuts onto a paper towel-lined plate to drain.
13. Meanwhile, for the frosting: in a bowl, add all the ingredients and beat until smooth.
14. Coat the doughnuts with the frosting and enjoy.

Nutritional Information:

Calories 7186.2; Fat 193.5g; Cholesterol 600.7mg; Sodium 4600.1mg; Carbohydrates 1238.6g; Protein 117.8g

CHAPTER 7: COCONUT BAKED RECIPES

1. CARIBBEAN AIR DONUTS

Preparation Time: 15 minutes
Cooking Time: 25 minutes
Servings: 1

Ingredients:

- 2 C. almond milk
- 2 tsp baking powder
- 2 tbsp sugar
- 1/2 C. thick coconut milk
- Powdered sugar

Directions:

1. In a bowl, add all the ingredients and mix until a dough forms.
2. Place the dough onto a floured surface and roll into 1/3-inch thickness.
3. Cut the rolled dough into long strips and then cut into diamonds.
4. In a deep skillet, add the oil and cook until heated through.
5. Add the dough diamonds in batches and cook until golden brown from both sides.
6. With a slotted spoon, transfer the dough diamonds onto a paper towel-lined plate to drain.
7. Coat the warm doughnuts with powdered sugar and enjoy.

Nutritional Information:

Calories 34.3; Fat 0.7g; Cholesterol 0.0mg; Sodium 20.7mg; Carbohydrates 6.1g; Protein 0.7g

2. SWEET CARROT DONUTS (GLUTEN-FREE)

Preparation Time: 30 minutes
Cooking Time: 38 minutes
Servings: 12

Ingredients:

- 1 1/2 tbsp ground flax seeds
- 1/4 C. hot water
- 1/3 C. All-purpose flour
- 1/3 C. Regular white flour
- 1/4 C. Cornstarch
- 1/2 tsp guar gum
- 3/4 tsp baking powder
- 1/2 tsp cinnamon
- 1/4 tsp nutmeg
- 1/4 tsp ginger
- 1/4 tsp salt
- 2 tbsp ground pecans
- 3 tbsp cream of rice
- 2 tbsp fine cornmeal
- 1/3 C. unsweetened vanilla almond milk
- 3 tbsp brown sugar
- 2 tbsp maple syrup
- 1 tbsp oil
- 1/2 tbsp vanilla
- 2/3 C. grated carrot
- 1/4 C. medium-shredded unsweetened coconut

Directions:

1. Set your oven to 425 degrees F before doing anything else, and lightly grease a doughnut pan.
2. In a bowl, add the hot water and flax and mix well.
3. Keep aside.

4. In a second bowl, add the cornstarch, flours, brown rice cereal, pecans, guar gum, baking powder, cinnamon, ginger, nutmeg, and salt and mix well.

5. In a third bowl, add the maple syrup, almond milk, oil, brown sugar, and vanilla and beat until well combined.

6. Add the flax mixture and beat until well combined.

7. Add the flour mixture and mix until well combined.

8. Gently fold in the coconut and carrots.

9. In the prepared doughnut holes, place the mixture evenly.

10. Cook in the oven for about 8 minutes.

11. Remove from the oven and place onto a wire rack to cool for about 5 minutes.

12. Carefully remove the doughnuts from the pan and enjoy.

Nutritional Information:

Calories 118.2; Fat 5.7g; Cholesterol 0.0mg; Sodium 81.7mg; Carbohydrates 15.9g; Protein 1.5g

3. CHAI DONUTS FOR EVENING CHAI

Preparation Time: 10 minutes
Cooking Time: 35 minutes
Servings: 16

Ingredients:

- 1 tsp cinnamon
- Eight eggs
- 1 cup warm water steeped in 4 chai bags
- 1 tsp vanilla extract
- 1 cup powdered Stevia
- ½ tsp sea salt
- ¾ cup coconut flour
- 2 tbsp butter
- 1 tsp baking powder

Ingredients for making vanilla glaze:

- 1 tsp vanilla extract
- 1 cup of coconut oil
- 1 cup powdered Stevia

Directions:

1. Keep the oven ready by preheating at 350 degrees.
2. Put the eggs in a bowl along with coconut oil and sweetener. Prepare the tea and then blend it with the other wet ingredients.
3. Mix the dry ingredients in another bowl and then blend it with the wet mixture. Pour the batter into a donut pan and then bake them for 30 minutes.
4. Make the vanilla glaze by mixing all the ingredients in a bowl and then spreading the donuts' glaze.

Nutritional Information:

Protein: 3g; Fat: 15g; Carbohydrate: 8.9g

4. SUPER TASTY DONUTS WITH SOUR CREAM

Preparation Time: 5 minutes
Cooking Time: 15 minutes
Servings: 10

Ingredients:

- ½ cup Stevia
- 1 cup sour cream
- 2/3 cup coconut flour
- ½ tsp sea salt
- Three large eggs
- 4 tbsp heavy cream
- ½ tsp vanilla
- ½ tsp baking powder
- ¾ cup melted butter

Directions:

1. You will have to mix the wet and dry ingredients separately and then blend them to make the donut batter.
2. The batter will be thick as pancake batter.
3. Grease the donut pan with butter and pour the batter with a spoon.
4. Bake at 300 degrees for 12 minutes, making sure that the donuts are golden brown.
5. Serve with your favorite dip or hot coffee.

Nutritional Information:

Protein: 2g; Fat: 28g; Carbohydrate: 2g

5. FLAVORFUL NUTTY DONUTS

Preparation Time: 5 minutes
Cooking Time: 30 minutes
Servings: 6

Ingredients:

- ½ cup Stevia
- 2 cups blanched wheat flour
- 1 tsp sea salt
- 1/8 tsp baking soda
- 1 tsp stevia glycerite
- 1¼ cups almond milk (unsweetened)
- ¼ tsp coconut extract
- 1 tsp almond extract
- Three large eggs3½ tsp baking powder
- ½ cup shredded coconut (unsweetened)

Directions:

1. Keep the oven ready by preheating at 350 degrees and grease the donut pan with cooking spray. Put all the ingredients in a blender and mix thoroughly.
2. Pour the batter into the donut wells and bake them for 25 minutes. Let them cool down on wire racks and then serve. You can also store them in airtight containers.

Nutritional Information:

Protein: 9g; Fat: 17g; Carbohydrate: 5.5g

6. CARIBBEAN AIR DONUTS

Preparation Time: 1 hours
Cooking Time: 2 hours

Ingredients

- 2 C. almond milk
- 2 tsp baking powder
- 2 tbsp sugar
- 1/2 C. thick coconut milk
- 2 tbsp powdered sugar

Directions

1. In a bowl, add all the ingredients and mix until a dough forms.
2. Place the dough onto a floured surface and roll into 1/3-inch thickness.
3. Cut the rolled dough into long strips and then cut into diamonds.
4. In a deep skillet, add the oil and cook until heated thoroughly.
5. Add the dough diamonds in batches and cook until golden brown from both sides.
6. With a slotted spoon, transfer the dough diamonds onto a paper towel-lined plate to drain.
7. Coat the warm doughnuts with the powdered sugar and enjoy.

Nutritional Information:

Calories 30.6; Fat 1g; Cholesterol 4mg; Sodium 20.7mg; Carbohydrates 17g; Protein 2g

CHAPTER 8: FRIED DOUGHNUT RECIPES

1. FLORIDA BUTTERMILK DONUTS

Preparation Time: 15 minutes
Cooking Time: 25 minutes
Servings: 1

Ingredients:

- Deep-frying oil
- 7 1/2 oz. buttermilk biscuits
- 4 tbsp sugar

Coating

- 2 C. powdered sugar
- 1/4 C. milk
- 1 tsp vanilla

Directions:

1. Carefully separate the dough into ten biscuits.
2. Then, with the cap of a bottle, cut a hole in the center of each biscuit.
3. In a deep skillet, add the oil and cook until its temperature reaches 350 degrees F.
4. Add the doughnuts in batches and cook for about 3 minutes, flipping once halfway through.
5. With a slotted spoon, transfer the doughnuts onto a paper towel-lined plate to drain.
6. Meanwhile, for the glaze: in a bowl, add the milk, powdered sugar, and vanilla and mix well.
7. Coat the warm doughnuts with sugar and then dip into glaze.
8. Enjoy.

Nutritional Information:

Calories 165.8; Fat 3.1g; Cholesterol0.8mg; Sodium 223.3mg; Carbohydrates 33.0g; Protein 1.6g

2. CUSTARD FILLED CRISPY DONUTS

Preparation Time: 6 minutes
Cooking Time: 15 minutes
Servings: 12

Ingredients:

- One egg
- ½ cup vanilla whey
- 2 tsp baking powder
- 4 tbsp vanilla-flavored almond milk
- ½ cup Stevia
- 1/8 tsp sea salt
- 12 tsp orange-flavored custard (for filling)
- Oil for frying

Directions:

1. Blend all the donut making ingredients in a bowl and use a hand blender to make the batter smooth.
2. Heat oil in a frying pan and fry 12 donuts in batches. When one side is browned, flip over to cook the other side.
3. Allow the donuts to cool down and then use a sharp knife to cut through the middle and then insert one teaspoon of custard in each one.

Nutritional Information:

Protein: 0.2g; Fat: 2.3g; Carbohydrate: 1g

3. DELIGHTFUL APPLE FLAVORED DONUTS WITH TWIST OF CINNAMON

Preparation Time: 5 minutes
Cooking Time: 12 minutes
Servings: 6

Ingredients for making apple flavored donuts:

- ½ tsp nutmeg
- ½ cup coconut flour
- 2 tbsp protein powder
- 1 tsp of Vanilla Essence
- ¼ tsp cornstarch
- 2 tsp baking powder
- ¼ tsp kosher salt
- ¼ cup granulated Stevia
- 1 tsp ground cinnamon
- Two eggs
- 1 tbsp melted butter
- ½ cup apple cider (non-alcoholic)

Ingredients for cinnamon coating:

- ¼ cup powdered Stevia
- 4 tbsp melted butter
- 1½ tsp ground cinnamon

Directions:

1. Mix the dry and wet ingredients in separate bowls and then blend them to make the donut dough. The dough must be a bit firm.
2. Now make six balls from the dough and shape them like classic donuts.
3. Heat oil in a frying pan and fry the donuts in batches, making sure they are well cooked and golden brown.
4. Mix the ground cinnamon with powdered Stevia to make the coating.
5. Use a brush to coat the donuts with melted butter, and then sprinkle the cinnamon mixture. Let them rest for a few minutes so that the cinnamon coating can cling well with the butter.
6. Serve as evening snacks

Nutritional Information:

Protein: 9g; Fat: 17g; Carbohydrate: 5.5g

CHAPTER 9: BAKED CINNAMON DOUGHNUT RECIPES

1. PARISIAN STYLE CINNAMON DONUTS

Preparation Time: 15 minutes
Cooking Time: 45 minutes
Servings: 14

Ingredients:

- 5 tbsp margarine
- 1/2 C. sugar
- One egg
- 1 1/2 C. flour
- 2 1/4 tsp baking powder
- 1/4 tsp salt
- 1/2 tsp nutmeg
- 1/2 C. milk
- 6 tbsp margarine, melted
- 3 tsp cinnamon
- 1 tbsp sugar

Directions:

1. Set your oven to 350 degrees F before doing anything else and grease 14 cups of muffin pans.
2. In a bowl, add the flour, baking powder, nutmeg, and salt and mix well.
3. In another bowl, add the sugar and margarine and beat until creamy.
4. Add the egg and beat until well combined.
5. Add the flour mixture, alternating with the milk, and mix until just combined.
6. Place the mixture into the prepared muffin cups about halfway full.
7. Cook in the oven for about 20-25 minutes.
8. Remove from the oven.
9. Then, immediately, remove the doughnuts from the pan.
10. Dip each doughnut into margarine and then coat it with cinnamon sugar.

Nutritional Information:

Calories 172.4; Fat 9.7g; Cholesterol 14.5mg; Sodium 214.1mg; Carbohydrates 19.4g; Protein 2.2g

2. CINNAMON WEDDING DONUTS

Preparation Time: 15 minutes
Cooking Time: 45 minutes
Servings: 36

Ingredients:

- 2 C. flour
- 3/4 C. sugar
- 2 tsp baking powder
- 3/4 C. milk
- 1 tsp salt
- Two eggs, beaten

- 1 tsp vanilla
- 1 tbsp shortening, melted
- 1/4 tsp nutmeg
- 1/4 tsp cinnamon
- 1 C. confectioners' sugar
- 2 tbsp water

Directions:

1. Set your oven to 325 degrees F before doing anything else, and lightly grease a mini doughnut pan.
2. In a bowl, add the flour, baking powder, sugar, and salt and mix well.
3. Add the milk, eggs, shortening, and vanilla and beat until well combined.
4. In the prepared doughnut holes, place the mixture about 2/3 full.
5. Cook in the oven for about 8 minutes.
6. Remove from the oven and keep aside to cool.
7. For the glaze: in a bowl, add the confectioners' sugar, nutmeg, cinnamon, and water and beat until well combined
8. Carefully remove the doughnuts from the pan.
9. Coat with the glaze and enjoy.

Nutritional Information:

Calories 65.4; Fat 0.9g; Cholesterol 12.4mg; Sodium 91.3mg; Carbohydrates 13.1g; Protein 1.2g

3. CLOVE DOUGHNUTS

Preparation Time: 15 minutes
Cooking Time: 35 minutes
Servings: 12

Ingredients

- Six egg whites
- 1 C. buttermilk
- 2 tsp Canola oil
- 1/2 C. whole wheat flour
- 1/2 C. almond milk
- 2/3 C. powdered sugar
- 1/4 tsp nutmeg, ground
- 1/4 tsp clove, ground
- 1/8 tsp mace
- 1/4 tsp cinnamon
- 1/4 C. powdered sugar

Directions:

1. Set your oven to 400 degrees F before doing anything else and lightly grease cups of a muffin pan.
2. In a bowl, add the egg whites and beat until frothy.
3. Add the oil and buttermilk and beat until well combined.
4. Add the flours, powdered sugar, mace, nutmeg, cinnamon, and cloves and beat until smooth.
5. In the prepared muffin cups, place the mixture evenly.
6. Cook in the oven for about 20 minutes.
7. Remove from the oven and place the pan onto a wire rack for about 1 minute.
8. Carefully remove the pan's doughnuts and keep them aside to cool for about 4-5 minutes.
9. Enjoy with a dusting of the powdered sugar.

Nutritional Information:

Calories 95.5; Fat 1.1g; Cholesterol 0.8mg; Sodium 49.4mg; Carbohydrates 17.9g; Protein 3.7g

4. PRE-COLONIAL DONUTS

Preparation Time: 10 minutes
Cooking Time: 20 minutes
Servings: 1

Ingredients:

- 1 C. sugar
- 4 tsp baking powder
- 1 1/2 tsp salt
- 1/2 tsp nutmeg
- Two eggs
- 1/4 C. unsalted butter, melted
- 1 C. milk
- 4 C. flour
- oil
- cinnamon sugar

Directions:

1. In a bowl, add the sugar, baking powder, nutmeg, and salt and mix well.
2. Add the melted butter, milk, and eggs and beat until well combined.
3. Add 3 C. of the flour and beat until well combined.
4. Add 1 C. of the flour and beat until a soft and sticky but firm dough forms.
5. With plastic wrap, cover the dough and place it in the fridge for about 2 hours.
6. Divide the dough into two portions.
7. Place the dough portions onto a floured surface and roll each into 1/2-inch thickness.
8. With a doughnut cutter, cut the circles from each dough portion.

9. With the cap of a bottle, cut a hole in the center of each doughnut.

10. In a deep skillet, add about 1-inch of oil and cook until its temperature reaches 360 degrees F.

11. Place the doughnuts in batches and cook for about 2-3 minutes, flipping occasionally.

12. With a slotted spoon, transfer the doughnuts onto a paper towel-lined plate to drain.

13. Coat with cinnamon sugar and enjoy.

Nutritional Information:

Calories 236.8; Fat 4.9g; Cholesterol 37.7mg; Sodium 372.8mg; Carbohydrates 42.7g; Protein 5.2g

5. LISA'S 10-MINUTE DROP DOUGHNUTS

Preparation Time: 5 minutes
Cooking Time: 10 minutes
Servings: 36

Ingredients:

- 2 C. sifted flour
- 1/3 C. sugar
- 3 tsp baking powder
- 1/2 tsp salt
- One egg, beaten
- 3/4 C. milk
- 3 tbsp oil
- Additional oil, if needed

Directions:

1. In a bowl, add the flour, baking powder, and salt and mix well.
2. Now, sift the flour mixture into another bowl.
3. Add the sugar and mix well.
4. In another bowl, add the egg, milk, and 3 tbsp of the oil and beat until well combined.
5. Add the flour mixture and mix until smooth.
6. In a deep skillet, add the oil and cook until its temperature reaches 365 degrees F.
7. With tsp, place the mixture and cook until golden brown, flipping occasionally.
8. With a slotted spoon, transfer the doughnuts onto a paper towel-lined plate to drain.
9. Coat with cinnamon sugar and enjoy.

Nutritional Information:

Calories 47.8; Fat 1.5g; Cholesterol 5.8mg; Sodium 67.1mg; Carbohydrates 7.4g; Protein 1.0g

6. ALLEGANY DONUT SQUARES

Preparation Time: 15 minutes
Cooking Time: 21 minutes
Servings: 1

Ingredients:

- 1 (1/4 oz.) package granular yeast
- 1/2 C. lukewarm water
- 1 tsp sugar
- 1/2 C. scalded milk
- 1/4 C. sugar
- 1/4 C. shortening
- 1 tsp salt
- 1 tsp cinnamon
- 1 C. raisins
- One egg
- 2 1/2-2 3/4 C. unsifted almond milk, divided

Glaze

- 2 tbsp honey
- 1/8 tsp salt
- 2 C. icing sugar
- 7 tbsp boiling water

Directions:

1. In a bowl, add 1/2 C. lukewarm water, 1 tsp of the sugar, and mix well.
2. Add the yeast and gently stir.
3. Keep aside for about 10 minutes.
4. Meanwhile, in a bowl, add the shortening, raisins, 1/4 C. of the sugar, cinnamon, salt, and mix until well combined.
5. Keep aside until cool to lukewarm.
6. Add egg and beat until well combined.
7. Add the yeast mixture and 2 1/4 C. of the flour and beat for about 5 minutes.
8. With plastic wrap, cover the bowl and keep aside in a warm area for about 2 hours.
9. With your hands, punch down the dough.
10. Now, place the dough onto a floured surface with the remaining flour, and with your hands, knead for about 10 minutes.
11. Roll the dough into the 1/3-inch thickness and then cut into 3-inch squares.
12. Keep aside, uncovered for at least 1 1/2 hours.
13. In a deep skillet, add the oil and cook until its temperature reaches 375 degrees F.
14. Add the doughnuts in batches and cook for about 1 1/2 minutes, flipping once halfway through.
15. With a slotted spoon, transfer the doughnuts onto a paper towel-lined plate to drain.
16. Meanwhile, for the glaze: in a bowl, add all the ingredients and mix until smooth.
17. Coat the warm doughnuts with the glaze and enjoy.

Nutritional Information:

Calories 3473.1; Fat 65.0g; Cholesterol 228.5mg; Sodium 2780.8mg; Carbohydrates 691.7g; Protein 49.9g

7. AKRON DROP DONUTS

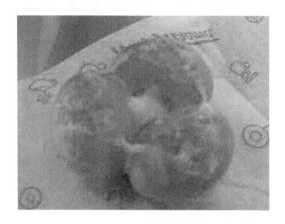

Preparation Time: 5 minutes
Cooking Time: 12 minutes
Servings: 1

Ingredients:

- 1 (18 1/4 oz.) packages wild blueberry muffin mix
- 1/2 C. flour
- 3/4 C. milk

- One egg
- shortening
- 1/2 C. sugar
- 1 tsp cinnamon

Directions:

1. In a bowl, add the flour and muffin mix and mix well.
2. Add the egg and milk and egg and mix until just combined.
3. Add the blueberries and gently stir to combine.
4. In a deep skillet, add the shortening and cook until its temperature reaches 365 degrees F.
5. With tsp, add the mixture in batches and cook until golden brown from both sides.
6. With a slotted spoon, transfer the doughnuts onto a paper towel-lined plate to drain.
7. Meanwhile, in a bowl, add the cinnamon and sugar and mix well.
8. Coat the warm doughnuts with cinnamon sugar and enjoy.

Nutritional Information:

Calories 901.5; Fat 21.3g; Cholesterol 79.0mg; Sodium 998.9mg; Carbohydrates 161.7g; Protein 14.7g

8. MATZO DONUTS

Preparation Time: 20 minutes
Cooking Time: 1 hour 20 minutes
Servings: 20

Ingredients:

- 2/3 C. water
- 1 tbsp sugar
- 1/4 tsp salt
- 1/2 C. oil
- 1 C. matzo meal
- Three eggs
- cinnamon-sugar mixture
- chopped nuts

Directions:

1. Set your oven to 375 degrees F before doing anything else and grease a baking sheet.
2. In a pan, add the oil, water, sugar, and salt and cook until boiling.
3. Add the matzo meal and stir to combine.
4. Remove from the heat and keep aside to cool slightly.
5. Add the eggs, one at a time, beating well after each addition.
6. With greased hands, make 2-inch balls from the dough.
7. Sprinkle the top of each ball with cinnamon sugar and nuts.
8. At the bottom of the prepared baking sheet, arrange the dough balls.
9. Cook in the oven for about 1 hour.
10. Enjoy warm.

Nutritional Information:

Calories 83.6; Fat 6.2g; Cholesterol 31.7mg; Sodium 41.3mg; Carbohydrates 5.3g; Protein 1.4g

9. VIRGINIA CORN DONUTS

Preparation Time: 5 minutes
Cooking Time: 10 minutes
Servings: 1

Ingredients:

- 2 2/3 C. almond milk
- 3/4 C. sugar
- 1 tsp baking soda
- 1 tsp salt
- Two eggs
- 1/2 C. sour cream
- 1/2 C. milk
- 1 tsp vanilla
- vegetable oil
- cinnamon sugar

Muffin mix

- ½ c + ½ tbsp white flour
- ½ c cornmeal
- 1 tbsp baking powder
- ½ tsp table salt
- 2 tbsp vegetable oil
- 2 tbsp white sugar

Directions:

1. Take a bowl and mix all ingredients of muffin mix.
2. Now, add the flour, muffin mix, sugar, baking soda, and salt and mix well.
3. Add the eggs, sour cream, milk, and vanilla and mix well.
4. Place the dough onto a cornmeal-lined smooth surface, and with your hands, pat it into 1/2-inch thickness.
5. Then, cut the dough into 16 equal-sized strips.
6. Shape the dough strips into doughnut circles.
7. In a deep skillet, add the oil and cook until its temperature reaches 325 degrees F.
8. Add the doughnuts in batches and cook for about 30-40 seconds, flipping once halfway through.
9. With a slotted spoon, transfer the doughnuts onto a paper towel-lined plate to drain.
10. Coat the warm doughnuts with cinnamon sugar and enjoy.

Nutritional Information:

Calories 205.2; Fat 4.4g; Cholesterol 30.9mg; Sodium 408.0mg; Carbohydrates 36.4g; Protein 4.4g

10. 20-MINUTE DONUT BISCUITS

Preparation Time: 10 minutes
Cooking Time: 25 minutes
Servings: 10

Ingredients:

- 2 (7 1/2 oz.) packages refrigerated buttermilk biscuits
- 1/2 C. butter, melted
- 1 C. sugar
- 4 tbsp cinnamon
- 10 tsp raspberry jam

Directions:

1. Set your oven to 375 degrees F before doing anything else and grease a baking sheet.
2. In a microwave-safe bowl, add the butter and microwave for about 45 seconds.
3. In a bowl, add the cinnamon and sugar and mix well.
4. Coat the edge of a biscuit with the melted butter and then with the cinnamon sugar.
5. At the bottom of the prepared baking sheet, arrange the biscuits.
6. Now, spread about 1/2 tsp of the jam in the center of each biscuit.
7. With your finger, make a little well in the center of each biscuit.
8. Cook in the oven for about 15 minutes.
9. Enjoy warm.

Nutritional Information:

Calories 319.5; Fat 15.0g; Cholesterol 24.4mg; Sodium 538.5mg; Carbohydrates 45.3g; Protein 2.8g

11. SOUTHERN DONUT PUDDING

Preparation Time: 20 minutes
Cooking Time: 2 hrs. 20 minutes
Servings: 20

Ingredients:

- 20 stale plain doughnuts, chopped
- 1-quart milk
- 12 eggs, beaten
- 2 C. sugar
- 1 tbsp sugar

- 1/2 C. raisins
- 2 tbsp vanilla
- 4 oz. butter
- 1 tbsp cinnamon

Directions:

1. Set your oven to 350 degrees F before doing anything else.
2. In a bowl, add the milk and eggs and beat until well combined.
3. Add the sugar, doughnuts, raisins, and vanilla and gently stir to combine.
4. In another bowl, add the cinnamon and sugar and mix well.
5. In 2 (9x13-inch) baking dishes, divide the mixture evenly.
6. Arrange the butter slices on top and dust with the cinnamon sugar.
7. With the pieces of foil, cover the baking dishes.
8. Cook in the oven for about 1 hour.
9. Remove the foil pieces and cook for about 45-60 minutes.
10. Enjoy.

Nutritional Information:

Calories 453.1; Fat 23.0g; Cholesterol 149.5mg; Sodium 304.3mg; Carbohydrates 53.0g; Protein 9.3g

12. AMISH DONUT HOLES

Preparation Time: 5 minutes
Cooking Time: 15 minutes
Servings: 4

Ingredients:

- 2 tbsp vegetable oil
- 3 tbsp granulated sugar
- 1/4 C. egg substitute
- 1 C. almond milk
- 1 1/2 tsp baking powder
- 1/4 tsp salt
- 4 tbsp low-fat milk
- 1/8 tsp nutmeg
- granulated sugar
- cinnamon sugar
- confectioners' sugar

Directions:

1. In a bowl, add the flour, sugar, baking powder, nutmeg, and salt and mix well.
2. In another bowl, add the milk, oil, and egg substitute and beat until well combined.
3. Add the flour mixture and mix until well combined.
4. In a deep skillet, add the oil and cook until its temperature reaches 375 degrees F.
5. With a tsp, add the mixture and cook until golden brown from both sides.
6. With a slotted spoon, transfer the doughnut holes onto a paper towel-lined plate to drain.
7. Coat the warm doughnuts with the confectioner's sugar and enjoy.

Nutritional Information:

Calories 225.0; Fat 7.2g; Cholesterol 0.7mg; Sodium 318.5mg; Carbohydrates 34.7g; Protein 5.2g

13. NO FRY DONUTS

Preparation Time: 10 minutes
Cooking Time: 35 minutes
Servings: 10

Ingredients:

- 1 3/4 C. flour
- 1 1/2 tsp baking powder
- 1/2 tsp salt
- 1/2 tsp ground nutmeg
- 1/4 tsp ground cinnamon
- 3/4 C. sugar
- 1/3 C. vegetable oil
- One egg, beaten
- 3/4 C. low-fat milk
- Jam

Coating

- 1/4 C. butter, melted
- 1/3 C. sugar
- 1 tsp ground cinnamon

Directions:

1. Set your oven to 350 degrees F before doing anything else and grease a muffin pan.
2. In a bowl, add the flour, baking powder, cinnamon, nutmeg, and salt and mix well.
3. In another bowl, add the milk, oil, sugar, and egg and beat until well combined.
4. Add the flour mixture and mix until just combined.
5. In the prepared muffin cups, place the mixture about 1/2 full and top each with 1 tsp of the jam.
6. Now, place the remaining mixture over the jam in each muffin cup about 3/4 of the full.
7. Cook in the oven for about 20-25 minutes.
8. Remove from the oven and keep onto the wire rack to cool in the pan for about 5 minutes.
9. Carefully invert the muffins onto the wire rack to cool completely.
10. In a bowl, place the melted butter.
11. In another bowl, add the sugar and cinnamon and mix well.
12. Immediately, dip the tops in butter and coat with cinnamon sugar.

Nutritional Information:

Calories 284.8; Fat 12.7g; Cholesterol 31.7mg; Sodium 227.1mg; Carbohydrates 39.7g; Protein 3.5g

14. DONUTS IN THE BREAD MACHINE II

Preparation Time: 20 minutes
Cooking Time: 2 hrs. 20 minutes
Servings: 1

Ingredients:

- Three medium potatoes, peeled and quartered
- 1 C. milk
- Two eggs, well beaten
- 3/4 C. shortening
- 1/2 C. sugar
- 1 tsp salt
- 4 1/2 C. bread flour
- 2 1/4 tsp active dry yeast
- Coating
- 3/4 C. sugar
- 1 1/4 tsp ground cinnamon
- 1/4 C. butter, melted

Directions:

1. In a pan of water, add the potatoes and cook until boiling.
2. Cook until cooked through.
3. Drain the potatoes, reserving 1/4 C. of the cooking water in a bowl.
4. Keep the liquid aside to cool to 70-80 degrees F.
5. With a potato masher, mash the potatoes entirely and place bout 1 C. in a bowl.
6. Keep aside at room temperature to cool.
7. In the bread machine pan, place the dough ingredients in order as suggested by the manual alongside 1 C. of the cooled mashed potatoes and reserved cooking water.
8. Select the Dough cycle.
9. After completing the cycle, transfer the dough onto a lightly floured surface and roll into 1/2-inch thickness.
10. With a two 1/2-inch doughnut cutter, cut the doughnuts.
11. In 2 greased baking sheets, arrange the doughnuts.
12. With plastic sheets, cover the baking sheets and keep them aside in a warm place for about 25 minutes.
13. Set your oven to 350 degrees F.
14. Cook in the oven for about 15-20 minutes.
15. Meanwhile, in a bowl, add the cinnamon and sugar and mix well.
16. Coat the warm doughnuts with butter and cinnamon sugar.

Nutritional Information:

Calories 186.9; Fat 7.5g; Cholesterol 19.3mg; Sodium 98.8mg; Carbohydrates 26.9g; Protein 3.1g

15. POTLUCK DONUTS

Preparation Time: 1 hour
Cooking Time: 2 hours
Servings: 5

Ingredients:

- 4 tbsp of melted butter
- 2 C. white sugar
- Two eggs
- 2 C. milk
- 2 tsp cream of tartar
- 1 tsp baking soda
- 4 tsp baking powder
- 1/2 tsp salt
- 1 1/2 tsp nutmeg
- 1/2 tsp cinnamon
- 7 -8 C. flour
- Sugar
- Oil

Directions:

1. In a bowl, add the flour, baking soda, baking powder, cream of tartar, nutmeg, cinnamon, and salt and mix well.
2. Now, sift the flour mixture into another bowl.
3. In another bowl, add the eggs, sugar, and butter and beat until creamy.
4. Add the flour mixture, alternating with the milk, and mix until well combined.
5. Place the dough onto a floured surface and roll into 1/4-inch thickness.
6. With a doughnut cutter, cut the doughnuts.
7. In a deep skillet, add the oil and cook until its temperature reaches 365 degrees F.
8. Add the doughnuts in batches and cook until golden brown from both sides.
9. With a slotted spoon, transfer the doughnuts onto a paper towel-lined plate to drain.
10. Coat the warm doughnuts with the sugar and enjoy.

Nutritional Information:

Calories 80.6; Fat 1.2g; Cholesterol 8.7mg; Sodium 65.7mg; Carbohydrates 15.7g; Protein 1.7g

16. ITALIAN BOARDWALK DONUTS

Preparation Time: 15 minutes
Cooking Time: 25 minutes
Servings: 24

Ingredients:

- One vanilla bean
- 1/2 C. sugar
- 3 tbsp sugar
- 2 tbsp ground cinnamon
- 1/2 C. butter
- 1/4 tsp salt
- 1 C. water
- 1 C. almond milk
- Four eggs
- Olive oil

Directions:

1. Open the vanilla bean lengthwise and then, with the back of a knife, scrape the seeds.
2. In a bowl, add the vanilla bean seeds, 1/2 C. of the sugar, and cinnamon and mix well.
3. In a pan, add the butter, 3 tbsp of the sugar, salt, and water over medium heat, and cook until boiling.

4. Remove from the heat and stir in the flour until well combined.

5. Again, place the pan over the heat and cook for about 4-5 minutes, mixing always.

6. Transfer the flour mixture into a bowl.

7. Add the eggs, one at a time, and with an electric hand mixer, beat on low speed until well combined and smooth.

8. In a deep skillet, add the oil and cook until its temperature reaches 375 degrees F.

9. With a small ice-cream scooper, add the mixture and cook for about 5 minutes, flipping once halfway through.

10. With a slotted spoon, transfer the doughnuts onto a paper towel-lined plate to drain.

11. Coat the warm doughnuts with cinnamon sugar and enjoy.

Nutritional Information:

Calories 88.8; Fat 4.7g; Cholesterol 45.4mg; Sodium 63.5mg; Carbohydrates 10.2g; Protein 1.6g

17. LULU'S LITTLE DONUTS

Preparation Time: 15 minutes
Cooking Time: 45 minutes
Servings: 1

Ingredients:

- 1 1/2 C. almond milk
- 3/4 C. sugar
- 2 tsp baking powder
- 1/4 tsp salt
- 1/4 tsp nutmeg
- One large egg
- 1/2 C. milk
- 1/2 C. melted butter
- 1/2 tsp vanilla
- 1/2 tsp ground cinnamon

Directions:

1. Set your oven to 350 degrees F before doing anything else and grease cups of a mini muffin pan.
2. In a bowl, add the flour, baking powder, 1/2 C. of the sugar, nutmeg, salt, and mix well.
3. In a second bowl, add the milk, egg, 1/4 C. of the melted butter, and vanilla and beat until well combined.
4. Add the flour mixture and mix until just combined.
5. In the prepared muffin cups, place the mixture evenly.

6. Cook in the oven for about 15 minutes.

7. Meanwhile, in a bowl, add the cinnamon and 1/3 C. of the sugar and mix well.

8. Coat the warm doughnut tops with 3 tbsp of the melted butter.

9. Coat with cinnamon sugar and enjoy.

Nutritional Information:

Calories 1122.5; Fat 51.7g; Cholesterol 236.3mg; Sodium 1047.7mg; Carbohydrates 151.4g; Protein 15.3g

18. YELLOW DONUTS

shutterstock.com • 210059431

Preparation Time: 10 minutes
Cooking Time: 22 minutes
Servings: 24

Ingredients:

- 1 C. sugar
- 1 1/2 tsp ground cinnamon
- 1 (18 1/4 oz.) packages cake mix
- 2 pinch yellow food color
- 1/8 C. water
- 1/2 C. vegetable oil
- Three eggs
- 1 tbsp ground nutmeg

Directions:

1. Set your oven to 350 degrees F before doing anything else and grease 24 cups of a mini muffin pan.
2. In a bowl, add the cinnamon and sugar and mix well.
3. In another bowl, add the cake mix, yellow tint, eggs, oil, and water, and mix as directed onto the package.
4. Add the nutmeg and stir to combine.
5. In the prepared muffin pan, place the mixture about 2/3 of the full.
6. Cook in the oven for about 12 minutes.
7. Coat warm doughnuts with the sugar mixture and enjoy.

Nutritional Information:

Calories 176.4; Fat 7.7g; Cholesterol 23.6mg; Sodium 150.9mg; Carbohydrates 25.5g; Protein 1.7g

19. SWEET DROPPED DONUTS IN PORTUGAL

Preparation Time: 30 minutes
Cooking Time: 50 minutes
Servings: 20

Ingredients:

- 1-quart water
- One lemon, zest
- One stick cinnamon
- 2 tbsp butter
- 4 C. flour
- 4 tsp baking powder
- 4 tbsp sugar
- 12 eggs
- 1 tsp salt

Directions:

1. In a pan, add the water, lemon rind, and cinnamon stick and cook until boiling.
2. Meanwhile, in a bowl, add the flour, sugar, baking powder, and salt and mix well.
3. Add the butter into the boiling water and stir until butter is melted completely.
4. Remove from the heat and discard the lemon rind and cinnamon sticks.
5. Place the water into the bowl of the flour mixture and beat vigorously until well combined.

6. Add eggs, one at a time, and beat well after each addition.

7. In a deep skillet, add the oil and cook until heated through.

8. With a spoon, add the mixture and cook until golden brown from both sides.

9. Add the doughnuts in batches and cook for about 2-4 minutes, flipping once halfway through.

10. With a slotted spoon, transfer the doughnuts onto a paper towel-lined plate to drain.

11. Coat the warm doughnuts with cinnamon sugar and enjoy.

Nutritional Information:

Calories 155.5; Fat 4.3g; Cholesterol 129.9mg; Sodium 240.5mg; Carbohydrates 22.0g; Protein 6.3g

20. MEXICAN DONUT HOLES

Preparation Time: 30 minutes
Cooking Time: 1 hour
Servings: 1

Ingredients:

- 2/3 C. sugar, divided
- 1 tsp ground cinnamon
- 1/4 C. butter, softened
- Two eggs
- 1 tsp vanilla extract
- 1 3/4 C. almond milk, divided
- 2 tsp baking powder
- 1 tsp salt
- 1/4 C. milk
- Vegetable oil

Directions:

1. In a bowl, add the cinnamon and 1/3 C. of the sugar and mix well.
2. Keep aside.
3. In another bowl, add the remaining 1/3 C. of the sugar and butter and an electric mixer; beat until creamy.
4. Add the eggs and vanilla and mix well.
5. Add 1 C. of the flour, baking powder, and salt and mix well
6. Add the flour mixture into the bowl of the milk mixture and mix well

7. Add the remaining flour and mix until a soft dough forms.

8. Place onto a floured surface and with your hands, knead for about 2 minutes.

9. With a lightly floured rolling pin, roll the dough into 1/4-inch thickness.

10. Place the dough onto a floured surface and roll into 1/4-inch thickness.

11. With a 2-inch round cookie cutter, cut the doughnuts.

12. In a deep skillet, add 2-inch of the oil over medium heat and cook until heated through.

13. Add the doughnuts in batches and cook for about 3-4 minutes, flipping once halfway through.

14. With a slotted spoon, transfer the doughnuts onto a paper towel-lined plate to drain.

15. Coat the warm doughnuts with cinnamon sugar and enjoy.

Nutritional Information:

Calories 641.5; Fat 19.9g; Cholesterol 167.5mg; Sodium 1211.6mg; Carbohydrates 102.9g; Protein 12.5g

21. CANDY DONUTS

Preparation Time: 10 minutes
Cooking Time: 10 minutes
Servings: 8

Ingredients:

- 9 C. oil
- 1 C. sugar
- 1/4 C. cinnamon
- 1 (16 oz.) cans icing
- candy sprinkles

Directions:

1. With the cap of a bottle, cut a hole in the center of each biscuit.
2. In a deep skillet, add the oil and cook until its temperature reaches 375 degrees F.
3. Add the doughnuts in batches and cook, covered for about 6 minutes, flipping once halfway through.
4. With a slotted spoon, transfer the doughnuts onto a paper towel-lined plate to drain.
5. Meanwhile, in a bowl, add the cinnamon and sugar and mix well.
6. Coat the warm doughnuts with cinnamon sugar, icing, and sprinkles, and enjoy.

Nutritional Information:

Calories 2457.4; Fat 253.0g; Cholesterol 0.5mg; Sodium 568.0mg; Carbohydrates 52.7g; Protein 3.9g

22. DOUGHNUTS TOSCANO

Preparation Time: 2 hrs.
Cooking Time: 2 hrs. 2 minutes
Servings: 1

Ingredients:

Dough

- 1 1/3 C. water
- 3 tsp sugar
- 1 tsp salt
- 2 tbsp olive oil
- 2 tbsp cornmeal
- 3 C. unbleached almond milk
- 1 tsp baking powder
- 1 1/2 tsp bread machine yeast

Donut

- vegetable oil
- olive oil
- 1 lb. prepared pizza dough
- 3/4 C. sugar
- 1 1/2 tsp ground cinnamon

Directions:

1. In the pan of a bread machine, place the dough ingredients in order as suggested by the manual.
2. Select the Dough cycle and press the Start button.
3. Place the dough onto a floured surface and roll into 1/2-inch thickness.
4. With a floured 2-inch cookie cutter, cut the doughnuts.
5. Then, with the cap of a bottle, cut a hole in the center of each doughnut.
6. In a deep skillet, add the same quantity of both oils over medium heat and cook until its temperature reaches 375 degrees F.
7. Add the doughnuts in batches and cook until golden brown from both sides.
8. Add the doughnuts in batches and cook for about 1 1/2 minutes, flipping once halfway through.
9. With a slotted spoon, transfer the doughnuts onto a paper towel-lined plate to drain.
10. Meanwhile, in a bowl, add the cinnamon and sugar and mix well.
11. Coat the warm doughnuts with cinnamon sugar and enjoy.

Nutritional Information:

Calories 193.3; Fat 2.6g; Cholesterol 0.0mg; Sodium 226.3mg; Carbohydrates 38.9g; Protein 3.5g

23. VANILLA ALMOND MILK DONUTS

Preparation Time: 8 minutes
Cooking Time: 16 minutes
Servings: 1

Ingredients:

- 2 C. flour
- 1/2 C. vegan sugar
- 2 tsp baking powder
- 1 1/2 tsp egg substitute
- 2 tbsp water
- 3/4 C. almond milk
- 1 tsp vanilla extract
- 4 tsp cooking oil
- cinnamon sugar

Directions:

1. Set your oven to 325 degrees F before doing anything else, and lightly grease a doughnut pan.
2. In a mug, add the egg substitute and water and mix well.
3. In a bowl, add the flour, baking powder, and sugar and mix well.
4. Add the oil, almond milk, egg substitute mixture, and vanilla and beat until well combined.
5. In the prepared doughnut holes, place the mixture evenly.
6. Cook in the oven for about 8-10 minutes.
7. Carefully remove the doughnuts from the pan.
8. Coat with cinnamon sugar and enjoy.

Nutritional Information:

Calories 82.0; Fat 1.1g; Cholesterol 0.0mg; Sodium 41.5mg; Carbohydrates 16.3g; Protein 1.4g

24. NEW HAMPSHIRE STYLE DONUTS

Preparation Time: 20 minutes
Cooking Time: 50 minutes
Servings: 24

Ingredients:

- 1 C. sour milk
- Four egg yolks
- 2 tbsp melted shortening
- 1/2 tsp vanilla
- 4 C. flour
- 1 tsp salt
- 1/2 tsp cream of tartar
- 3/4 C. sugar
- 1/2 tsp nutmeg
- 1 tsp cinnamon
- 3/4 tsp baking soda
- Oil

Directions:

1. In a bowl, add the flour, baking soda, cinnamon, nutmeg, and salt and mix well.
2. Now, sift the flour mixture into a second bowl.
3. In another bowl, add the egg yolks and beat until lemon colored.

4. Add the sugar and beat until well combined.
5. Add the shortening, milk, cream of tartar, and vanilla and beat until well combined.
6. Add the flour mixture and mix until a sticky dough forms.
7. Place the dough onto a floured surface and roll into 3/4-inch thickness.
8. With a doughnut cutter, cut the doughnuts.
9. In a deep skillet, add the oil and cook until its temperature reaches 350 degrees F.
10. Add the doughnuts in batches and cook until golden brown from both sides.
11. With a slotted spoon, transfer the doughnuts onto a paper towel-lined plate to drain.
12. Coat the warm doughnuts with powdered sugar and enjoy.

Nutritional Information:

Calories 124.8; Fat 2.3g; Cholesterol 28.6mg; Sodium 142.3mg; Carbohydrates 22.8g; Protein 2.8g

CHAPTER 10: BEST DOUGHNUT RECIPES WORLDWIDE

1. MILANESE CHEESE DONUTS

Preparation Time: 15 minutes
Cooking Time: 25 minutes
Servings: 24

Ingredients:

- One egg, beaten
- 1 tbsp sugar
- 1 C. almond milk
- 3 tbsp milk
- 2 tsp baking powder
- 1 C. ricotta cheese
- Vegetable oil

Directions:

1. In a bowl, add all the ingredients and mix until well combined.
2. In a deep skillet, add the oil and cook until heated through.
3. With a tsp, add the mixture and cook until golden brown from both sides.
4. With a slotted spoon, transfer the doughnuts onto a paper towel-lined plate to drain.
5. Dust with the powdered sugar and enjoy.

Nutritional Information:

Calories 43.2; Fat 1.6g; Cholesterol 13.2mg; Sodium 42.8mg; Carbohydrates 5.0g; Protein 2.0g

2. TRUE AMERICAN DONUT

Preparation Time: 40 minutes
Cooking Time: 50 minutes
Servings: 1

Ingredients:

- 7 1/2 C. sugar
- 3/4 C. lard
- Nine eggs
- 3 (8 oz.) cans evaporated milk
- 3 (8 oz.) cans of water
- 18 C. flour
- 18 tsp baking powder
- 7 1/2 tsp salt
- 9 tsp nutmeg

Directions:

1. In a bowl, add the flour, baking powder, nutmeg, and salt and mix well.
2. Now, sift the flour mixture into another bowl.
3. In another bowl, add the lard and sugar and beat until creamy.
4. Add the eggs and beat until well combined.
5. Add the evaporated milk and water and beat until well combined.
6. Add the flour mixture and mix until a stiff dough forms.
7. Place the dough onto a floured surface and roll into 1/2-inch thickness.
8. With a doughnut cutter, cut the doughnuts.
9. In a deep skillet, add the oil and cook until heated through.
10. Add the doughnuts in batches and cook until golden brown from both sides.
11. With a slotted spoon, transfer the doughnuts onto a paper towel-lined plate to drain.
12. Enjoy warm.

Nutritional Information:

Calories 68.4; Fat 1.1g; Cholesterol 8.9mg; Sodium 101.5mg; Carbohydrates 13.2g; Protein 1.3g

3. GERMAN CREAM FILLED DONUTS

Preparation Time: 30 minutes

Cooking Time: 40 minutes

Servings: 18

Ingredients :

One package of active dry yeast

- 1/4 C. warm water
- 1/2 C. whipping cream
- 1/3 C. softened butter
- 2 tbsp sugar
- One egg
- 2 C. almond milk

Cream Filling

- 2/3 C. whipping cream
- 1 tbsp almond milk
- 1 tbsp sugar
- 1 tsp vanilla
- One egg yolk
- Hot fat
- Powdered sugar

Directions:

1. In a bowl, add the warm water and yeast and mix until well combined.
2. Keep aside for about 5 minutes.
3. Add the butter, whipping cream, egg, and sugar and beat until well combined.
4. Add 1 C. of the flour and whisk until smooth.
5. Slowly, add the remaining flour and whisk until smooth.
6. With plastic wrap, cover the bowl and keep aside for about 30 minutes.
7. Again beat until smooth.
8. Keep aside for about 30 minutes.
9. Meanwhile, for the filling: In a heavy-bottomed pot, add all the ingredients over medium heat and cook until boiling.
10. Cook for about 5 minutes, stirring frequently.
11. Remove from the heat and keep aside to cool.
12. Place the dough onto a lightly floured surface.
13. Make a ball from the dough and then roll it into an 18-inch square.
14. Place the filling onto half of the dough about 3 inches apart.
15. Fold the other half of the dough over the filling.
16. With a C., cut the cakes, and with your fingers, press the edges to seal.
17. Place the puffs onto a lightly floured piece of waxed paper and keep them aside for about 30-40 minutes.
18. In a deep skillet, add the oil and cook until its temperature reaches 375 degrees F.
19. Add the doughnuts in batches and cook until golden brown from both sides.
20. With a slotted spoon, transfer the doughnuts onto a paper towel-lined plate to drain.
21. Coat the warm doughnuts with powdered sugar and enjoy.

Nutritional Information:

Calories 152.1; Fat 9.7g; Cholesterol 52.4mg; Sodium 34.9mg; Carbohydrates 13.6g; Protein 2.4g

4. DOUGHNUTS LEVIATHAN

Preparation Time: 1 hour 30 minutes
Cooking Time: 1 hour 32 minutes
Servings: 24

Ingredients:

- 3/4 C. sugar
- 1/2 C. oil
- 2 (1/4 oz.) package yeast
- Two eggs, beaten
- 2 tsp salt
- 3 C. water
- 1 tsp nutmeg
- 8 C. flour

Directions:

1. In a bowl, add 1 C. of the warm water and yeast and mix well.
2. In another bowl, add the oil, 2 C. of the hot water, eggs, flour, sugar, nutmeg, salt, and mix until well combined.
3. Add the remaining flour and yeast mixture and mix until well combined.
4. With plastic wrap, cover the bowl and keep it aside in a warm area for about 1 1/2 hours.
5. Place the dough onto a floured surface and roll into 1/2-inch thickness.
6. With a doughnut cutter, cut the doughnuts.

7. In the bottom of 2 floured baking sheets, arrange the doughnuts and keep them aside in a warm area for about 30 minutes.
8. In a deep skillet, add the oil and cook until heated through.
9. Add the doughnuts in batches and cook until golden brown from both sides.
10. With a slotted spoon, transfer the doughnuts onto a paper towel-lined plate to drain.
11. Enjoy warm.

Nutritional Information:

Calories 224.4; Fat 5.4g; Cholesterol 17.6mg; Sodium 201.3mg; Carbohydrates 38.3g; Protein 5.0g

5. DOUGHNUTS SASKATOON SASKATCHEWAN STYLE

Preparation Time: 20 minutes
Cooking Time: 25 minutes
Servings: 1

Ingredients:

- 2 C. sugar
- 2 tsp salt
- 6 tbsp corn oil
- Four eggs
- 2 1/4 C. buttermilk

- 8 C. flour
- 8 tsp baking powder
- 1 tsp baking soda
- One pinch ginger
- 1 tsp nutmeg

Directions:

1. In a bowl, add all the ingredients and mix until well combined.
2. Place the dough onto a floured surface and with your hands, kneed until a non-sticky dough forms.
3. With a rolling pin, roll the dough into 1/4-inch thickness.
4. With a doughnut cutter, cut the doughnuts.
5. In a deep skillet, add the oil and cook until its temperature reaches 400 degrees F.
6. Add the doughnuts in batches and cook until golden brown from both sides.
7. With a slotted spoon, transfer the doughnuts onto a paper towel-lined plate to drain.
8. Enjoy warm.

Nutritional Information:

Calories 248.9; Fat 2.6g; Cholesterol 36.1mg; Sodium 403.8mg; Carbohydrates 50.0g; Protein 6.1g

6. DOUGHNUTS BRASILEIRO

Preparation Time: 10 minutes
Cooking Time: 35 minutes
Servings: 1

Ingredients:

- 1 C. almond milk
- 1/2 C. cornstarch
- 2 tsp baking powder
- 1/2 C. milk
- Two eggs
- 2 -3 green onions, chopped
- 1 tsp salt
- oil

Directions:

1. In a bowl, add the corn starch, flour, and baking powder and mix well.
2. In another bowl, add the eggs, green onions, and salt and beat well.
3. Add the flour mixture, alternating with the milk, and mix until a thick mixture is formed.
4. In a deep skillet, add the oil and cook until its temperature reaches 350 degrees F.
5. With a tbsp, add the mixture in batches and cook for about 3-4 minutes, flipping once halfway through.
6. With a slotted spoon, transfer the doughnuts onto a paper towel-lined plate to drain.
7. Enjoy warm.

Nutritional Information:

Calories 37.3; Fat 0.6g; Cholesterol 15.5mg; Sodium 130.6mg; Carbohydrates 6.5g; Protein 1.2g

7. SPANISH DOUGHNUTS

Preparation Time: 1 hour 30 minutes
Cooking Time: 2 hrs.
Servings: 1

Ingredients:

- 2 (1/4 oz.) package each active dry yeast
- 1/2 C. warm water
- 1 1/2 C. warm milk
- Five eggs, beaten
- 5 tbsp sugar
- 1/4 C. butter, softened
- 1/2 tsp salt
- 5 -5 1/2 C. almond milk
- Oil
- Granulated sugar

Directions:

1. In a bowl, add the warm water and yeast and mix until well combined.
2. Add the butter, milk, eggs, sugar, and salt and beat until smooth.
3. Add enough flour and mix until a soft dough forms.
4. In a greased bowl, place the dough and turn to coat the top.
5. With plastic wrap, cover the bowl and keep it aside in a warm area for about 1 hour.
6. In a deep skillet, add the oil and cook until its temperature reaches 375 degrees F.
7. With a tbsp, add the mixture and cook for about 3-4 minutes, flipping once halfway through.
8. With a slotted spoon, transfer the doughnuts onto a paper towel-lined plate to drain.
9. Coat the warm doughnuts with the granulated sugar and enjoy.

Nutritional Information:

Calories 791.8; Fat 20.0g; Cholesterol 245.1mg; Sodium 472.4mg; Carbohydrates 125.4g; Protein 25.3g

8. JAPANESE DONUTS

shutterstock.com • 1780695278

Preparation Time: 10 minutes
Cooking Time: 40 minutes
Servings: 12

Ingredients:

- Oil
- Four eggs
- 3/4 C. milk
- 3/4 tsp vanilla
- 4 C. flour
- 2 C. sugar
- 3 1/2 tbsp baking powder
- 1/4 tsp salt

Directions:

1. In a bowl, add the flour, baking powder, sugar, and salt and mix well.
2. Now, sift the flour mixture into another bowl.
3. In another bowl, add the milk, eggs, and vanilla and beat until well combined.
4. Add the flour mixture and mix until a smooth dough forms.
5. In a deep skillet, add the oil and cook until its temperature reaches 350 degrees F.
6. With a tsp, place the mixture and cook until golden brown from both sides.
7. With a slotted spoon, transfer the doughnuts onto a paper towel-lined plate to drain.
8. Enjoy hot.

Nutritional Information:

Calories 317.7; Fat 2.6g; Cholesterol 72.6mg; Sodium 397.8mg; Carbohydrates 66.9g; Protein 6.9g

9. DONUTS RHODE ISLAND STYLE

Preparation Time: 20 minutes
Cooking Time: 40 minutes
Servings: 1

Ingredients:

- 1 (1/4 oz.) package dry active yeast
- 1/4 C. warm water
- 3/4 C. warm milk
- 1/4 C. sugar
- 1 tsp salt
- One egg
- 1/4 C. shortening
- 3 1/2-3 3/4 C. almond milk

Directions:

1. In a bowl, add the warm water and yeast and mix until well combined.
2. Add the shortening, milk, egg, 2 C. of the flour, sugar, and salt and mix until well combined.
3. Add the remaining flour and mix until a dough forms.
4. Place the dough onto a lightly floured surface and with your hands, knead until smooth and elastic.
5. In a lightly greased bowl, place the dough and turn to coat evenly.
6. With a damp cloth, cover the bowl and keep it aside in a warm area for about 1 1/2 hours.
7. With your hands, punch down the dough and With a damp cloth, cover the bowl and keep it aside in a warm area for about 30 minutes.
8. Place the dough onto a floured surface and roll into 3/8-inch thickness.
9. With a doughnut cutter, cut the doughnuts.

10. Keep aside for about 30 minutes.
11. In a deep skillet, add the oil and cook until its temperature reaches 375 degrees F.
12. Add the doughnuts in batches and cook until golden brown from both sides.
13. With a slotted spoon, transfer the doughnuts onto a paper towel-lined plate to drain.
14. Enjoy warm.

Nutritional Information:

Calories 1225.3; Fat 33.7g; Cholesterol 105.8mg; Sodium 1250.4mg; Carbohydrates 197.8g; Protein 30.1g

10. JAPANESE DONUT

Preparation Time: 20 Minutes
Cooking Time: 28 Minutes

Ingredients

- 1/4 C. butter, softened
- 1 C. sugar
- 2 tbsp confectioners' sugar
- 2 large egg yolks, Beaten
- 1 large egg, Beaten

- 4 C. unbleached flour
- 2 tsp baking powder
- 1/4 tsp nutmeg
- 1/2 tsp baking soda
- 3/4 C. buttermilk

Directions

1. In a bowl, add the flour, baking powder, baking soda, nutmeg and salt and mix well.
2. Now, sift the flour mixture into another bowl.
3. In another bowl, add the sugar and butter and beat until creamy.
4. Add the whole egg and egg yolks and beat until well combined.
5. Add the flour mixture, alternating with the buttermilk and mix until well combined.
6. In a deep skillet, add the oil and cook until its temperature reaches to 375 degrees F.
7. With a tsp, place the mixture and cook until golden brown from both sides.
8. With a slotted spoon, transfer the doughnuts onto a paper towel-lined plate to drain.
9. Enjoy hot.

Nutritional Information:

Calories 326.5; Fat 6.6g; Cholesterol 76.0mg; Sodium 197.1mg; Carbohydrates 59.4g; Protein 6.9g

CHAPTER 11: BONUS DOUGHNUT RECIPES

1. MY FIRST SPUDNUT

Preparation Time: 5 minutes
Cooking Time: 10 minutes
Servings: 4

Ingredients:

- 1/2 C. potato, mashed with milk and butter
- One egg, beaten
- 1/2 C. sour cream
- 1/4 C. sugar
- 1/2 tsp vanilla extract
- 1 1/2 C. almond milk
- 1/2 tsp baking soda
- 1/4 tsp baking powder
- cooking oil
- confectioners' sugar

Directions:

1. In a bowl, add the flour, baking soda, and baking powder, and mix well.
2. Add the flour mixture and mix until well combined.
3. Add the flour mixture and mix until well combined.
4. In a deep skillet, add the oil and cook until its temperature reaches 375 degrees F.
5. Add the doughnuts in batches and cook for about 2 minutes, flipping once halfway through.
6. With a slotted spoon, transfer the doughnuts onto a paper towel-lined plate to drain.
7. Coat the warm doughnuts with the sugar and enjoy.

Nutritional Information:

Calories 308.4; Fat 7.3g; Cholesterol 61.4mg; Sodium 223.0mg; Carbohydrates 52.6g; Protein 7.3g

2. LEMON DONUTS

Preparation Time: 30 minutes
Cooking Time: 1 hour 10 minutes
Servings: 1

Ingredients:

- 3/4 C. butter
- 3 C. sugar
- Eight eggs, beaten
- Two lemons, zest
- 1 tsp lemon flavoring

- 9 -9 1/2 C. almond milk, divided
- 1/2 tsp salt
- 1 tsp baking soda
- 2 tsp cream of tartar
- oil

Directions:

1. In a bowl, add 4 C. of the flour, baking soda, cream of tartar, and salt and mix well.
2. In another bowl, add the sugar and butter and beat until creamy.
3. Add the eggs, lemon flavoring, and lemon zest and mix well.
4. Add the flour mixture and mix until well combined.
5. Add the remaining flour, 1 C. at a time, and mix until a very stiff dough form.
6. With your hand, roll the dough into 1-inch-thick snake-like rolls.
7. Then, cut each roll into 2-inch long fingers.
8. Place in the fridge for a whole night.
9. In a deep skillet, add the oil and cook until heated through.
10. Add the dough fingers in batches and cook until golden brown from both sides.
11. Add the doughnuts in batches and cook for about 2-4 minutes, flipping once halfway through.
12. Enjoy.

Nutritional Information:

Calories 71.6; Fat 1.6g; Cholesterol 17.9mg; Sodium 34.6mg; Carbohydrates 12.7g; Protein 1.4g

3. ALL-PURPOSE DONUT

Preparation Time: 20 minutes
Cooking Time: 2 hrs. 20 minutes
Servings: 20

Ingredients:

- 1 1/2 C. milk
- 2 1/2 oz. vegetable shortening
- 2 1/2 tbsp instant yeast
- 1/3 C. warm water
- Two eggs, beaten
- 1/4 C. sugar
- 1 1/2 tsp salt
- 1 tsp nutmeg
- 23 oz. almond milk
- peanut oil

Directions:

1. In a pot, add the milk over medium heat and cook until just warmed.
2. In a bowl, add the shortening and top with the warm milk.
3. Keep aside.
4. In another bowl, add the warm water and sprinkle with the yeast.
5. Keep aside for about 5 minutes.

6. In the bowl of a stand mixer, attached with the paddle attachment, add the yeast mixture, eggs, lukewarm milk mixture, sugar, half of the flour, nutmeg, and salt and beat on low speed until combined.
7. Now, increase the speed to medium and beat until well combined.
8. Add the remaining flour and mix at low speed.
9. Now, increase the speed to medium and beat until well combined.
10. Now, set the mixer to the dough hook attachment and beat on medium speed until a smooth dough forms.
11. Place the dough into a generously greased bowl.
12. Cover the bowl and keep aside in a warm place for about 1 hour.
13. Place the dough onto a generously floured surface and roll into 3/8-inch thickness.
14. With a two 1/2-inch doughnut cutter, cut the doughnuts.
15. Then, with the cap of a bottle, cut a hole in the center of each doughnut.
16. In the bottom of a floured baking sheet, arrange the doughnuts.
17. With a tea towel, cover the baking sheet lightly and keep aside for about 30 minutes.
18. In a deep skillet, add the oil and cook until its temperature reaches 375 degrees F.
19. Add the doughnuts in batches and cook for about 2 minutes, flipping once halfway through.
20. With a slotted spoon, transfer the doughnuts onto a paper towel-lined plate to drain.
21. Keep aside to cool for about 15-20 minutes.
22. Enjoy.

Nutritional Information:

Calories 184.7; Fat 5.1g; Cholesterol 23.7mg; Sodium 191.8mg; Carbohydrates 29.0g; Protein 5.2g

4. DOUGHNUTS IN JULY

Preparation Time: 3 hrs.
Cooking Time: 3 hrs. 30 minutes
Servings: 1

Ingredients:

- 2 C. scalded milk
- 1/2 C. butter
- 2/3 C. sugar, divided
- 1 tsp salt
- 2 tbsp yeast
- Four eggs, beaten
- 1/4 tsp nutmeg
- 7 C. sifted flour

Coating

- 3 C. powdered sugar
- 1/2 tsp salt
- 1/2 tsp vanilla
- 1/2 C. cold water

Directions:

1. For the glaze: in a bowl, add all the ingredients and mix until well combined.
2. Keep aside.
3. In a pan, add the hot milk and butter and mix until butter is melted completely.
4. Add 1 tbsp of the sugar and salt and mix well.
5. Keep aside to cool.
6. After cooling, add the eggs, remaining sugar, 3 C. of the flour, yeast, nutmeg, and mix until well combined.
7. Add the remaining flour and mix until a sticky dough forms.
8. Now, with your hands, knead for about 5 minutes.
9. Keep aside for about 1-1 1/2 hours.
10. Place the dough onto a floured surface and roll it into the desired thickness.
11. Cut the dough into desired sized shapes.
12. Keep aside for about 30-45 minutes.
13. In a deep skillet, add the oil and cook until its temperature reaches 365 degrees F.
14. Add the doughnuts in batches and cook for about 2-4 minutes, flipping once halfway through.
15. With a slotted spoon, transfer the doughnuts onto a paper towel-lined plate to drain.
16. Coat the warm doughnuts with the glaze and enjoy.

Nutritional Information:

Calories 137.5; Fat 2.9g; Cholesterol 22.0mg; Sodium 101.3mg; Carbohydrates 24.8g; Protein 2.9g

5. 30-MINUTE DONUT DROP

Preparation Time: 20 minutes
Cooking Time: 28 minutes
Servings: 10

Ingredients:

- 1/4 C. butter, softened
- 1 C. sugar
- Two large egg yolks, Beaten
- One large egg, Beaten
- 4 C. unbleached flour

- 2 tsp baking powder
- 1/4 tsp nutmeg
- 1/2 tsp baking soda
- 3/4 C. buttermilk
- confectioners' sugar

Directions:

1. In a bowl, add the flour, baking powder, baking soda, nutmeg, and salt and mix well.
2. Now, sift the flour mixture into another bowl.
3. In another bowl, add the sugar and butter and beat until creamy.
4. Add the whole egg and egg yolks and beat until well combined.
5. Add the flour mixture, alternating with the buttermilk, and mix until well combined.
6. In a deep skillet, add the oil and cook until its temperature reaches 375 degrees F.
7. With a tsp, place the mixture and cook until golden brown from both sides.
8. With a slotted spoon, transfer the doughnuts onto a paper towel-lined plate to drain.
9. Enjoy hot.

Nutritional Information:

Calories 326.5; Fat 6.6g; Cholesterol 76.0mg; Sodium 197.1mg; Carbohydrates 59.4g; Protein 6.9g

6. VANILLA CRÈME DONUTS

Preparation Time: 2 hrs.
Cooking Time: 2 hrs. 5 minutes
Servings: 12

Ingredients:

- 1 (1/4 oz.) package quick-rising yeast
- 1/8 C. tap water, warm
- 3/4 C. milk, lukewarm scalded, then cooled
- 1/4 C. sugar
- 1/2 tsp salt
- One egg
- 1/4 C. shortening
- 2 1/2 C. almond milk

Filling

- 1/4 C. vegetable shortening
- 1/4 C. butter
- 1/2 tsp clear vanilla extract
- 2 C. sifted confectioners' sugar
- 1 tbsp evaporated milk

Directions:

1. In a bowl, add the warm water and yeast and mix until well combined.
2. Add the egg, milk, shortening, 1 C. of the flour, sugar, and salt, and with an electric mixer, beat on low speed for about 30 seconds.
3. Set the speed on medium and beat for about 2 minutes.
4. Add the remaining flour and mix until smooth.
5. With plastic wrap, cover the bowl and keep it aside in a warm area for about 50-60 minutes.
6. Place the dough onto a floured surface and roll into 1/2-inch thickness.
7. With a round cookie cutter, cut the doughnuts.
8. In the bottom of 2 floured baking sheets, arrange the doughnuts.
9. With plastic wrap, cover the bowl and keep it aside in a warm area for about 30-40 minutes.
10. In a deep skillet, add the oil and cook until its temperature reaches 350 degrees F.
11. Add the doughnuts in batches and cook until golden brown from both sides.
12. With a slotted spoon, transfer the doughnuts onto a paper towel-lined plate to drain.
13. Meanwhile, for the filling: in a bowl, add the shortening and butter and beat until creamy.
14. Slowly, add the sugar, 1/2 cup at a time, and beat until well combined.
15. Add the milk and vanilla and beat until light and fluffy.
16. Make a small hole in the center of each cooled doughnut.
17. Fill each doughnut with the filling generously and enjoy with a dusting of the confectioners' sugar.

Nutritional Information:

Calories 318.1; Fat 13.7g;Cholesterol 28.1mg; Sodium 146.8mg; Carbohydrates 45.1g; Protein 4.0g

7. HOT VANILLA DONUTS

Preparation Time: 25 minutes
Cooking Time: 35 minutes
Servings: 18

Ingredients:

- 2 (1/4 oz.) envelope active dry yeast
- 1/4 C. warm water
- 1 1/2 C. lukewarm milk
- 1/2 C. white sugar
- 1 tsp salt
- Two eggs
- 1/3 C. shortening
- 5 C. almond milk
- 1-quart vegetable oil
- Coating
- 1/3 C. butter
- 2 C. confectioners' sugar
- 1 1/2 tsp vanilla
- 4 tbsp hot water

Directions:

1. In a bowl, add the warm water and sprinkle with the yeast.
2. Keep aside for about 5 minutes.
3. In another bowl, add 2 C. of the flour, yeast mixture, milk, eggs, shortening, sugar, and salt with an electric mixer, beat on low speed until well combined.
4. Add the remaining flour, 1/2 C. at a time, and mix until a non-sticky dough forms.
5. Now, with your hands, knead the dough until smooth and elastic.
6. In a greased bowl, place the dough.
7. With a plastic sheet, cover the dough and keep it in a warm area until doubled in bulk.
8. Place the dough onto a floured surface and roll into 1/2-inch thickness.
9. With a floured doughnut cutter, cut the doughnuts.
10. In a deep skillet, add the oil and cook until heated through.
11. Add the doughnuts in batches and cook until golden brown from both sides.
12. With a slotted spoon, transfer the doughnuts onto a paper towel-lined plate to drain.
13. For the glaze: In a pot, add the butter over medium heat and cook until melted.
14. Add the confectioners' sugar and vanilla and stir until smooth.
15. Remove from the heat and stir in hot water until the desired consistency is achieved.
16. Coat the warm doughnuts with the glaze and enjoy.

Nutritional Information:

Calories 716.1; Fat 57.3g; Cholesterol 32.5mg; Sodium 178.6mg; Carbohydrates 46.7g; Protein 5.3g

8. DONUTS IN THE BREAD MACHINE I

Preparation Time: 15 minutes
Cooking Time: 55 minutes
Servings: 1

Ingredients:

- 1 1/4 C. milk
- One beaten egg
- 1/4 C. shortening
- 1/4 C. sugar
- 1 tsp salt
- 3 1/2 C. white flour
- 1 1/2 tsp dry yeast

Directions:

1. In a bread machine pan, place all the ingredients in order as suggested by the manual.
2. Select the Dough cycle and press the Start button.
3. Place the dough onto a floured surface and roll into 1/2-inch thickness.
4. With a 2-1/2-inch doughnut cutter, cut the doughnuts.
5. Then, with the cap of a bottle, cut a hole in the center of each doughnut.
6. With a kitchen towel, covered the doughnuts and keep aside for about 30 minutes.
7. In a deep skillet, add the oil and cook until its temperature reaches 375 degrees F.

8. Add the doughnuts in batches and cook until golden brown from both sides.

9. With a slotted spoon, transfer the doughnuts onto a paper towel-lined plate to drain.

10. Coat the warm doughnuts with the sugar and enjoy.

Nutritional Information:

Calories 1262.6; Fat 35.9g; Cholesterol 114.3mg; Sodium 1279.1mg; Carbohydrates 200.4g; Protein 31.9g

9. SIMPLE SOUR DONUTS

Preparation Time: 10 minutes
Cooking Time: 15 minutes
Servings: 10

Ingredients:

- 1 C. sour cream
- 1 C. granulated sugar
- Two large eggs
- 1 tsp baking soda
- 1/2 tsp salt
- 3 C. almond milk
- 1/8-1/4 tsp nutmeg
- 1 tsp vanilla extract
- Icing sugar

Directions:

1. In a bowl, add the flour, baking soda, nutmeg, and salt and mix well.
2. In another bowl, add the sugar and sour cream and beat well.
3. Add the eggs and beat until well combined.
4. Add the flour mixture and mix well.
5. Place the dough onto a floured surface and roll into 3/4-inch thickness.
6. With a doughnut cutter, cut the doughnuts.

7. In a deep skillet, add the oil and cook until its temperature reaches 370 degrees F.
8. Add the doughnuts in batches and cook until golden brown from both sides.
9. With a slotted spoon, transfer the doughnuts onto a paper towel-lined plate to drain.
10. Sprinkle the warm doughnuts with the icing sugar and enjoy.

Nutritional Information:

Calories 273.8; Fat 5.8g; Cholesterol 49.1mg; Sodium 275.7mg; Carbohydrates 49.4g; Protein 5.6g

10. DONUTS IN OSLO

Preparation Time: 24 hrs.
Cooking Time: 24 hrs. 10 minutes
Servings: 10

Ingredients:

- Three eggs
- 3/4 C. sugar
- 2/3 C. whipping cream
- 2/3 C. sour cream
- 3 C. flour
- 2 tbsp baking powder
- 1 tsp cardamom
- 2 tbsp butter, melted

Directions:

1. In a bowl, add the flour, baking powder, and cardamom and mix well.
2. Now, sift the flour mixture into another bowl.
3. In a second bowl, add the sour cream and whipping cream and beat until whipped.
4. In a third bowl, add the sugar and eggs and beat until light and fluffy.
5. Add the flour mixture, alternating with the cream mixture and gently, stir to combine.
6. Refrigerate overnight.
7. Place the dough onto a floured surface and roll into a 1-inch thickness.
8. With a doughnut cutter, cut the doughnuts.
9. In a deep skillet, add the oil and cook until its temperature reaches 350 degrees F.
10. Add the doughnuts in batches and cook until golden brown from both sides.
11. With a slotted spoon, transfer the doughnuts onto a paper towel-lined plate to drain.
12. Enjoy warm.

Nutritional Information:

Calories 322.7; Fat 13.0g; Cholesterol 91.6mg; Sodium 278.6mg; Carbohydrates45.4g; Protein 6.4g

11. CARDAMOM DONUTS

Preparation Time: 20 minutes
Cooking Time: 50 minutes
Servings: 15

Ingredients:

- Eight eggs
- 2 C. sugar
- 8 C. flour
- 1/2 C. butter, melted
- 1/2 C. whipping cream
- 1/8 tsp baking powder
- 1 tsp baking soda
- juice & zest of one lemon
- 2 tbsp cognac, optional
- Sugar
- Cardamom
- Oil

Directions:

1. In a bowl, add the eggs and beat until lemon colored.
2. Add the flour, sugar, baking soda, baking powder, whipping cream, butter, Cognac, lemon juice, and zest and mix until a stiff dough forms.
3. Keep the dough aside overnight.
4. Place the dough onto a floured surface and roll into 1/4-inch thickness.
5. With a doughnut cutter, cut the doughnuts.

6. In a deep skillet, add the oil over medium-high heat and cook until heated through.
7. In a deep skillet, add the oil and cook until its temperature reaches 350 degrees F.
8. Add the doughnuts in batches and cook until golden brown from both sides.
9. With a slotted spoon, transfer the doughnuts onto a paper towel-lined plate to drain.
10. In a bowl, mix the sugar and cardamom.
11. Coat the warm doughnuts with the sugar mixture and enjoy.

Nutritional Information:

Calories 466.7; Fat 12.3g; Cholesterol 139.9mg; Sodium 172.1mg; Carbohydrates 77.9g; Protein 10.4g

12. FRIENDSHIP DONUTS

Preparation Time: 30 minutes
Cooking Time: 30 minutes
Servings: 1

Ingredients:

- Three eggs
- 6 C. flour
- 2 C. warm water
- 2 tbsp salt
- 4 tbsp yeast
- 1/2 C. sugar
- 1/2 C. lard
- Coating
- 2 tsp white Karo
- 1 tsp vanilla
- 1 1/2 C. powdered sugar
- 2 -3 tbsp hot water

Directions:

1. In a large bowl, add 2 C. of the warm water and yeast and mix until well combined.
2. Add the flour, eggs, lard, sugar, and salt and mix until well combined.
3. With a tea towel, cover the dough and keep aside in a warm place until doubled in bulk.
4. Place the dough onto a floured surface and roll into 1/2-inch thickness.
5. With a doughnut cutter, cut the doughnuts.
6. With a tea towel, cover the dough and keep it aside in a warm place for about 30-45 minutes.

7. In a deep skillet, add the oil and cook until heated through.
8. Add the doughnuts in batches and cook until golden brown from both sides.
9. With a slotted spoon, transfer the doughnuts onto a paper towel-lined plate to drain.
10. Meanwhile, for the glaze: in a bowl, add the powdered sugar, Karo syrup, vanilla, and 2 tbsp of the hot water and mix until well combined.
11. Coat the warm doughnuts with the glaze and enjoy.

Nutritional Information:

Calories 143.2; Fat 3.5g; Cholesterol 20.3mg; Sodium 395.0mg; Carbohydrates 24.5g; Protein 3.1g

13. SWEET DINNER ROLL DONUTS

Preparation Time: 20 minutes
Cooking Time: 30 minutes
Servings: 4

Ingredients:

- 2 C. vegetable oil
- 1 Pack, any sweet biscuit
- 1 C. vanilla mix
- 2 tbsp caramel sauce
- 1/4 tsp kosher salt
- 1/2 C. powdered sugar
- Milk
- Additional caramel sauce

Directions:

1. Add milk in vanilla mix in a saucepan. Stir it over medium flame until in it thickens. Remove the pan when pudding is ready and bublles are formed.
2. Separate the crescent dough into four rectangles and press the holes tightly to seal.
3. Arrange two rectangles onto a smooth surface.
4. Top each with another rectangle.
5. Now, fold each stack in half widthwise.

6. With a 3-inch biscuit cutter, cut 1 round from each stack and then, with a 1/2-inch biscuit cutter, cut a small hole in the center of each game.

7. Reroll the remaining dough from both stacks and make a third doughnut in the same way.

8. In a deep skillet, add the oil and cook until its temperature reaches 325 degrees F.

9. Add the doughnuts in batches and cook until golden brown from both sides.

10. Add the doughnuts and cook for about 5 minutes, flipping once halfway through.

11. With a slotted spoon, transfer the doughnuts onto a paper towel-lined plate to drain.

12. Keep aside to cool for about 5 minutes.

13. Carefully cut each doughnut in half.

14. In a piping bag, fitted with a tip, place the pudding.

15. Pipe half of the pudding onto the bottom half of each doughnut and top each with some caramel sauce and salt.

16. Cover each bottom half with the top of the doughnut.

17. For the glaze: in a bowl, add the powdered sugar and enough milk and mix until the desired consistency is achieved.

18. Coat the top of each doughnut with the laze.

19. Enjoy with a drizzling of the caramel sauce.

Nutritional Information:

Calories 1259.2; Fat 113.7g; Cholesterol 29.0mg; Sodium 483.2mg; Carbohydrates 57.7g; Protein 5.9g

14. BROWNIE STYLE DONUTS FOR KETOGENIC DIETERS

Preparation Time: 3 minutes
Cooking Time: 15 minutes
Servings: 12

Ingredients for making brownie style donuts:

- ¼ cup of cocoa powder
- 12 tbsp butter
- ¾ cup Stevia
- ½ tsp vanilla extract
- Five eggs
- 4 oz unsweetened chocolate
- Ingredients for making chocolate ganache:
- Chocolate bar
- 2 tbsp butter

Directions:

1. Keep the oven ready by preheating at 325 degrees and grease the donut pan's coat with cooking spray.
2. Melt the butter and chocolate and cocoa powder in a saucepan over low heat, and then add the vanilla extract and Stevia. Allow cooling for a few minutes, and then whisk in the eggs.
3. Pour the batter into the donut pan and bake for 11 minutes.
4. In the meantime, make the chocolate ganache by mixing melted chocolate with butter and when the donuts are ready, spread the ganache over them and allow enough time to set.

Nutritional Information:

Protein: 4.8g; Fat: 6g; Carbohydrate: 3.8g

15. SUPER TASTY & HEALTHY ZUCCHINI DELIGHT

Preparation Time: 3 minutes
Cooking Time: 30 minutes
Servings: 6

Ingredients:

- Two eggs
- 1 cup blanched wheat flour
- ½ tsp cinnamon
- ¼ tsp sea salt
- ½ tsp baking soda
- 1/3 cup Stevia
- ½ cup chopped walnuts
- ¾ cup zucchini (grated)
- 1 tbsp butter
- ¼ cup unsweetened cocoa powder
- 1 tbsp almond milk

Directions:

1. Keep the oven ready by preheating at 350 degrees and grease the donut pan with cooking spray.
2. Mix the dry ingredients in a bowl, and then add the eggs, sweeteners, butter, and almond milk and the grated zucchini.
3. Finally, add the chopped walnuts to the batter and make sure that they are evenly distributed.
4. Pour the batter into the donut pan and bake them for 26 minutes. Allow cooling down in the wire rack and then serve.

Nutritional Information:

Protein: 9.2g; Fat: 19.3g; Carbohydrate: 7.7g

16. JELLY DONUTS

Preparation Time: 1 hours
Cooking Time: 1 hours 4 Minutes

Ingredients

- 2 (1/4 oz.) envelope dry yeast
- 6 tbsp shortening
- 1/4 C. warm water
- 5 C. flour
- 1 1/2 C. lukewarm milk
- 2 tbsp oil
- 3/4 C. sugar
- 1 (13 1/2 oz.) jar strawberry jelly
- 1 tsp salt
- 2 tbsp confectioners' sugar
- 2 eggs

Directions

1. In a bowl, add the warm water and sprinkle with the yeast.
2. Keep aside for about minutes.
3. In a bowl, add the 2 C. of the flour, yeast mixture, sugar, salt, milk, shortening, sugar and eggs and with an electric mixer; beat on low speed until well combined.
4. Add the remaining flour, 1/2 C. at a time and mix until a non-sticky dough forms.

5. With your hands, knead until smooth and elastic dough forms.

6. In a greased bowl, place the dough.

7. With a plastic wrap, cover the dough and keep in a warm place for about 1 hour.

8. Place the dough onto a floured surface and roll into 1/2-inch thickness.

9. With a doughnut cutter, cut the doughnuts.

10. Keep aside until doubled in size.

11. In a deep skillet, add 4 C. of the oil and cook until its temperature reaches to 350 degrees F.

12. 1Add the doughnuts in batches and cook until golden brown from both sides.

13. 1Add the doughnuts in batches and cook for about 2-4 minutes

14. With a slotted spoon, transfer the doughnuts onto a paper towel-lined plate to drain.

15. With a pastry injector, fill each doughnut with the jelly evenly.

16. Coat with the confectioners' sugar and enjoy.

Nutritional Information:

Calories 124.0; Fat 2.6g; Cholesterol 10.5mg; Sodium 69.5mg; Carbohydrates 22.8g; Protein 2.3g

17. DONUT BISCUITS

Preparation Time: 10 Minutes
Cooking Time: 25 Minutes

Ingredients

- 2 (7 1/2 oz.) packages refrigerated
- 4 buttermilk biscuits
- 1/2 C. butter, melted
- 1 C. sugar
- 4 tbsp cinnamon
- 10 tsp raspberry jam

Directions

1. Set your oven to 375 degrees F before doing anything else and grease a baking sheet.
2. In a microwave-safe bowl, add the butter and microwave for about 45 seconds.
3. In a bowl, add the cinnamon and sugar and mix well.
4. Coat the edge of a biscuit with the melted butter and then with the cinnamon sugar.
5. In the bottom of the prepared baking sheet, arrange the biscuits.
6. Now, spread about 1/2 tsp of the jam in the center of each biscuit.
7. With your finger, make a little well in the center of each biscuit.
8. Cook in the oven for about 15 minutes.
9. Enjoy warm.

Nutritional Information:

Calories 319.5; Fat 15.0g; Cholesterol 24.4mg; Sodium 538.5mg; Carbohydrates 45.3g; Protein 2.8g

18. CHEESE DONUTS

Preparation Time: 15 Minutes
Cooking Time: 25 Minutes

Ingredients

- 1 egg, beaten
- 1 tbsp sugar
- 1 C. almond milk
- 3 tbsp milk
- 2 tsp baking powder
- 1 C. ricotta cheese
- 2 tbsp vegetable oil

Directions

1. In a bowl, add all the ingredients and mix until well combined.
2. In a deep skillet, add the oil and cook until heated thoroughly.
3. With a tsp, add the mixture and cook until golden brown from both sides.
4. With a slotted spoon, transfer the doughnuts onto a paper towel-lined plate to drain.
5. Dust with the powdered sugar and enjoy.

Nutritional Information:

Calories 43.2; Fat 1.6g; Cholesterol 13.2mg; Sodium 42.8mg; Carbohydrates 5.0g; Protein 2.0g

19. DONUT HOLES

Preparation Time: 5 Minutes
Cooking Time: 15 Minutes

Ingredients

- 2 tbsp vegetable oil
- 1/8 tsp nutmeg
- 3 tbsp granulated sugar
- 2 tbsp granulated sugar
- 1/4 C. egg substitute
- 2 tbsp cinnamon sugar
- 1 C. almond milk
- 2 tbsp confectioners' sugar
- 1 1/2 tsp baking powder
- 1/4 tsp salt
- 4 tbsp low-fat milk

Directions

1. In a bowl, add the flour, sugar, baking powder, nutmeg and salt and mix well.
2. In another bowl, add the milk, oil and egg substitute and beat until well combined.
3. Add the flour mixture and mix until well combined.
4. In a deep skillet, add the oil and cook until its temperature reaches to 375 degrees F.
5. With a tsp, add the mixture and cook until golden brown from both sides.
6. With a slotted spoon, transfer the doughnut holes onto a paper towel-lined plate to drain.
7. Coat the warm doughnuts with the confectioner's sugar and enjoy.

Nutritional Information:

Calories 225.0; Fat 7.2g; Cholesterol 0.7mg; Sodium 318.5mg; Carbohydrates 34.7g; Protein 5.2g

20. SOUR DONUTS

Preparation Time: 10 Minutes
Cooking Time: 15 Minutes

Ingredients

- 1 C. sour cream
- 1 tsp vanilla extract
- 1 C. granulated sugar
- 2 tbsp icing sugar
- 2 large eggs
- 1 tsp baking soda
- 1/2 tsp salt
- 3 C. almond milk
- 1/8-1/4 tsp nutmeg

Directions

1. In a bowl, add the flour, baking soda, nutmeg and salt and mix well.
2. In another bowl, add the sugar and sour cream and beat well.
3. Add the eggs and beat until well combined.
4. Add the flour mixture and mix well.
5. Place the dough onto a floured surface and roll into 3/4-inch thickness.
6. With a doughnut cutter, cut the doughnuts.
7. In a deep skillet, add the oil and cook until its temperature reaches to 370 degrees F.
8. Add the doughnuts in batches and cook until golden brown from both sides.
9. With a slotted spoon, transfer the doughnuts onto a paper towel-lined plate to drain.
10. Sprinkle the warm doughnuts with the icing sugar and enjoy.

Nutritional Information:

Calories 273.8; Fat 5.8g; Cholesterol 49.1mg; Sodium 275.7mg; Carbohydrates 49.4g; Protein 5.6g

CONCLUSION

Congratulations! You made it till the end. Here you go with 100+ delicious and finger-licking doughnut recipes for you to try. The ball is in your court to try first whichever recipe appeased you the most.

Don't be afraid to mix and match flavors. The recipes can be interesting as evening snacks and also to fill your stomach anytime when you feel hungry. Most of the recipes provided here are simple but tasty. You can make them with ease as a beginner too.

These also make fantastic gifts, so make sure to share them with your friends, family, and co-workers.

GLOSSARY

Apple extract: Used to add flavor

Skillet: A metal frying pan with long handle

Stevia: A type of artificial sweetener

Whey protein powder: Used as an alternate of egg whites

INDEX

Made in the USA
Las Vegas, NV
01 December 2022

60550196R00109